Jillian Snee:
Juicing for Beginners

Copyright

Legal Disclaimer

Table of content

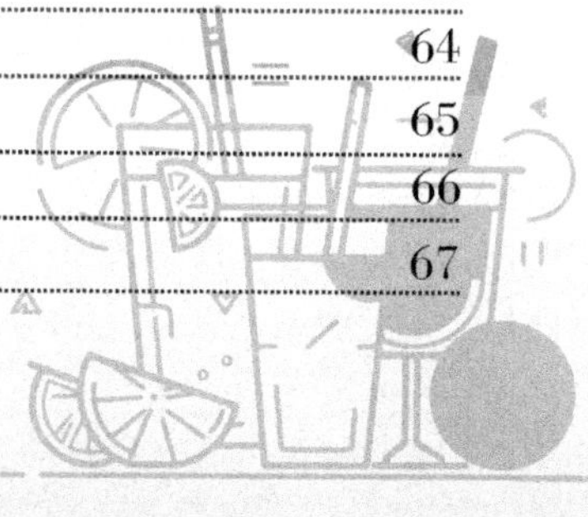

Introduction

The Journey to Fresh Juicing

The allure of fresh juicing is not just a passing trend; it's a return to nature's most potent elixirs. Imagine the first humans wandering ancient forests and meadows, instinctively crunching on berries, fruits, and herbs. This primal connection is embedded in our DNA, urging us towards natural wellness. Fast forward to today, amidst the cacophony of fast food commercials and instant gratifications, that same primal urge seeks solace, a return to authenticity. Fresh juicing is that bridge between then and now. When you take a sip of freshly made juice, it's not just nutrition you're imbibing but a legacy of natural wellness. Each drop is a tribute to the simplicity of nature and its bounty. In a world overwrought with complexity, juicing takes us on a journey back to basics, a path that resonates with our very essence. It's more than just a drink; it's an experience, a momentary escape, and a step closer to the purity that our souls often yearn for in the chaos of modern living.

Why Focus on Weight and Well-being?

Dive deep into any culture, and you'll find rituals, traditions, and foods that celebrate the human body. Our ancestors revered the human form, understanding that our body is not just a physical entity but a vessel of experiences, emotions, and life itself. In contemporary times, the emphasis on weight often overshadows the larger picture: holistic well-being. The scales tell a story, not just of our physical weight but our emotional baggage, our stress levels, our joys, and our traumas. When we speak of weight, we aren't merely addressing the pounds or kilograms but the entirety of our experiences.

This is where the role of juicing becomes pivotal. By focusing on health through fresh juices, we're not just addressing the weight in its physical sense but the weight of our emotions, our thoughts, and our spirits. The interdependence between weight and overall well-being is profound. A balanced diet and mindset can pave the way for emotional equilibrium, and conversely, a happy heart can lead to healthier food choices. It's a symbiotic relationship where one fuels and uplifts the other.

The Transformative Potential of Fresh Blends

Transformation is an all-encompassing journey, one that begins from within and radiates outwards. When we talk about fresh blends and their transformative power, it's not just about the external changes but the internal metamorphosis. Each blend, crafted with care and knowledge, is a promise to your body and soul. With every gulp, you're not just taking in nutrients but a commitment to change, growth, and evolution. Picture this: a world where every morning begins with a burst of nature's goodness, where midday slumps are replaced with vibrant energy, and where nights are restful and rejuvenating. Fresh blends offer more than mere sustenance; they provide an experience, a moment of mindfulness, and a bond with nature. As you progress through this guide, you'll not only discover recipes but a new perspective on life, health, and happiness. By integrating these juices into your daily ritual, you're setting forth on a journey of discovery, not just of flavors but of yourself.

As we embark on this voyage, let it be known that every page turned and every blend tried is a testament to your commitment to a healthier, more vibrant self. Here's to new beginnings, to health, and to the boundless potential within.

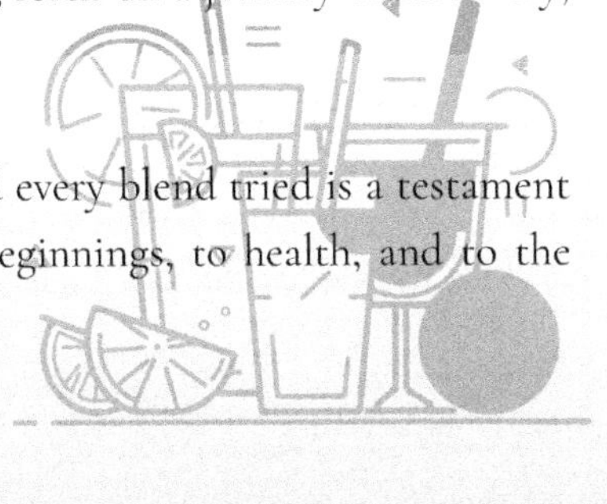

The Foundations of Juicing

Understanding Ingredients

The world of juicing presents a vast canvas of vibrant colors, textures, and flavors. When you begin to appreciate the unique qualities of each ingredient, you're not just consuming a drink but imbibing nature's finest extracts tailored for optimal health. This section meticulously breaks down the core components used in juicing, providing insights into their nutritional profiles and synergistic effects when combined.

Fruits: Nutritional Powerhouses

Nature's candy, as they're fondly called, fruits are reservoirs of essential vitamins, minerals, and bioactive compounds. While citrus fruits like oranges and grapefruits burst with immune-boosting vitamin C, berries come loaded with antioxidants that combat free radicals. Bananas contribute potassium, which is vital for heart health, and apples, with their abundant fiber, assist in digestive processes. Diversifying your fruit intake ensures you tap into a broad spectrum of nutritional benefits.

Vegetables: Unsung Heroes of Juicing

Beyond the appealing hues and flavors of fruits, vegetables lie at the heart of juicing, offering a treasure trove of nutrients. Dark leafy greens, such as kale and spinach, are abundant sources of iron and folate, essential nutrients for the body. Beets, with their sweet, earthy flavor, increase blood flow, while cucumbers, packed with hydrating properties, promote skin health by providing silica. Then there's broccoli, a cruciferous wonder packed with compounds that support detoxification processes and cellular health.

Herbs and Spices: Adding Flavor and Health Benefits

To relegate herbs and spices solely to culinary realms would be a vast underestimation. Incorporating them into juices can profoundly transform both the taste and health quotient of your drink. Herbs like basil offer adaptogenic properties, helping the body combat stress. Mint refreshes and aids digestion, while cilantro is known to bind with heavy metals, aiding in their removal from the body. Spices, on the other hand, are therapeutic powerhouses. Turmeric's active compound, curcumin, is an anti-inflammatory agent. Ginger soothes digestion and enhances metabolism.

Equipment Essentials

Embarking on a juicing journey requires the right set of tools. The efficiency, quality, and nutritional retention of your juice are significantly influenced by the equipment you choose.

Selecting the Right Juicer for You

Selecting the ideal juicer isn't just about pressing fruits and vegetables and collecting the juice. It's a journey to find a machine that aligns with your lifestyle, juicing preferences, and budget. The market offers a myriad of choices, each with its unique features and benefits.

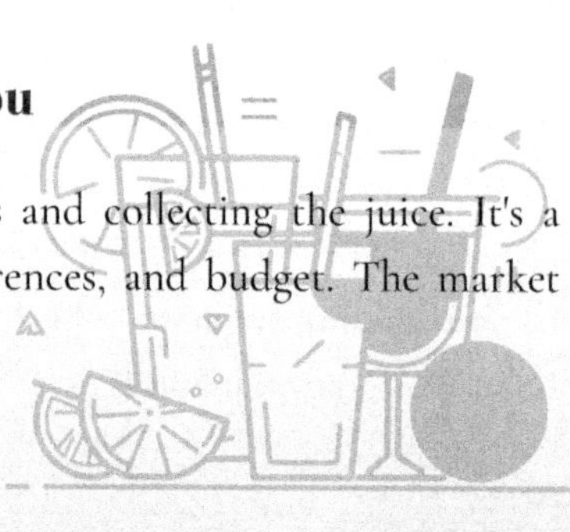

Centrifugal juicers, for instance, are the most common and budget-friendly. They work at high speeds, making them perfect for those always on the move. However, they can be a tad noisy and might not extract juice as efficiently as other types.

Masticating juicers, or cold press juicers, work slowly, crushing produce to extract juice. While they take a bit longer, they often yield more juice and retain more nutrients due to less heat exposure.

Triturating juicers use twin gears to crush and press produce. They're considered top-tier, especially for green leafy vegetables. Their efficacy comes with a higher price tag, but serious juicers often find it worthwhile.

Beyond the type, consider factors like ease of cleaning, size, noise level, and warranty. Your perfect juicer is out there, waiting to revolutionize your health journey. Invest time in understanding your needs, and you'll find a match that serves you for years to come.

Maintenance, Storage, and Care

The journey to optimal health through juicing doesn't end once you've concocted your perfect blend. Proper maintenance, storage, and care of your juicer and its components play a pivotal role in ensuring its longevity and performance. A well-maintained juicer will yield better-tasting juices, reduce chances of malfunction, and safeguard your health.

Maintenance: After each use, disassemble your juicer and rinse the parts under running water. This prevents pulp and juice residues from drying, which can be harder to remove later. For parts with crevices, use a cleaning brush, usually provided with your juicer. Occasionally, run a mixture of water and a mild detergent through the juicer to cleanse it internally.

Storage: Always ensure your juicer is completely dry before storing to prevent mold growth and unpleasant odors. If space allows, it's best to leave it assembled on the counter, ready for use. But if you need to stow it away, ensure it's placed in a dry, cool area, away from direct sunlight.

Care: Handle the juicer's components with care, especially the mesh strainer and any plastic parts, as they can be delicate. Periodically inspect the machine for wear and tear. The motor should run smoothly without emitting strange noises or odors. Lubricate any moving parts if the manufacturer recommends it. For optimal functionality, replace worn-out blades or screens.

Storing juices requires thought too. Freshly extracted juice starts to lose its nutritional value over time due to oxidation. Consume immediately, or store in an airtight container in the fridge for up to 24 hours.

Remember, the longevity of your juicer doesn't solely depend on its build quality but also on how you care for it. A little attention to detail can ensure that your juicer remains a staple in your health journey for years to come.

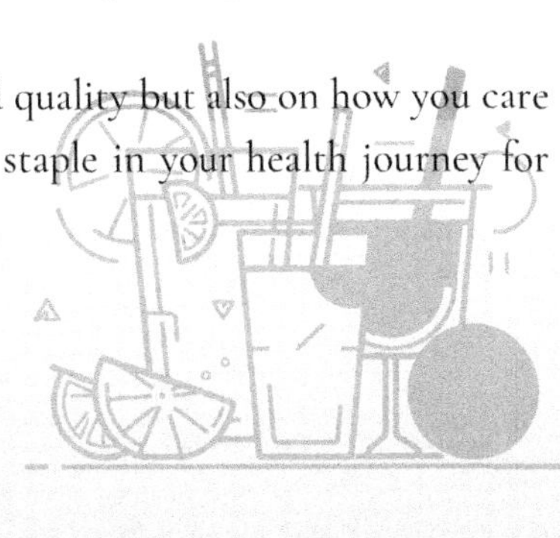

Building a Happy, Healthy Lifestyle with Juicing

How Juicing Impacts Mental and Physical Health

Juicing, a delightful alchemy of nature's best, goes beyond mere nutrition, weaving profound effects on both our minds and bodies. When we consume natural, unprocessed juices, we're essentially inviting an abundance of bioavailable nutrients into our system, ensuring rapid absorption.

Physically, the benefits are instantly palpable. You might experience heightened energy levels, smoother digestion, enhanced detoxification, and a clearer complexion. These positive changes often translate to improved endurance during physical activities and more restful sleep patterns.

Mentally, the influx of nutrients can have transformative effects. Think of the brain as an engine and the vitamins, minerals, and antioxidants you consume as the premium fuel. Regular intake of fresh juices can potentially sharpen cognitive functions, uplift mood, reduce mental fatigue, and even mitigate the effects of stress and anxiety. Moreover, the very act of dedicating time to nourish oneself through juicing can instill a sense of self-care and mindfulness, contributing to overall mental well-being.

Ingredients with Natural Mood Boosters

The intrinsic relationship between nutrition and mood is vast. While some ingredients stimulate the release of neurotransmitters associated with happiness, others reduce inflammation or oxidative stress that might otherwise hamper mood. Here's an enhanced exploration:

- **Berries** (Blueberries, Strawberries, Raspberries): Berries, particularly blueberries, have shown potential in increasing positive mood markers. Their bioactive compounds not only fight off brain aging but also enhance neural signaling, helping improve mood and memory.
- **Kale**: Beyond vitamins, kale boasts a treasure trove of mood-enhancing minerals like manganese, which has a pivotal role in the production of enzymes that act as mood stabilizers.
- **Spinach**: Spinach's richness in iron ensures optimal neurotransmitter synthesis. An iron-deficient diet might lead to feelings of lethargy and moodiness.
- **Bananas**: In addition to their neurotransmitter-producing components, bananas have a natural sugar balance of glucose, fructose, and sucrose, offering a quick energy boost and mood elevation.
- **Beets**: Along with betaine, beets are packed with tryptophan, a precursor for serotonin, often termed the 'feel-good' neurotransmitter.
- **Chia Seeds**: Aside from omega-3 fatty acids, chia seeds have a high concentration of alpha-linolenic acid (ALA), which has been associated with enhanced mood and a reduction in depressive symptoms.
- Citrus Fruits: Apart from vitamin C, they contain flavonoids that possess anti-inflammatory properties, potentially offering mood-enhancing benefits by reducing brain inflammation.
- Pumpkin Seeds: Apart from magnesium, they also contain L-tryptophan, which enhances the production of serotonin, offering a calming effect and improving sleep quality.

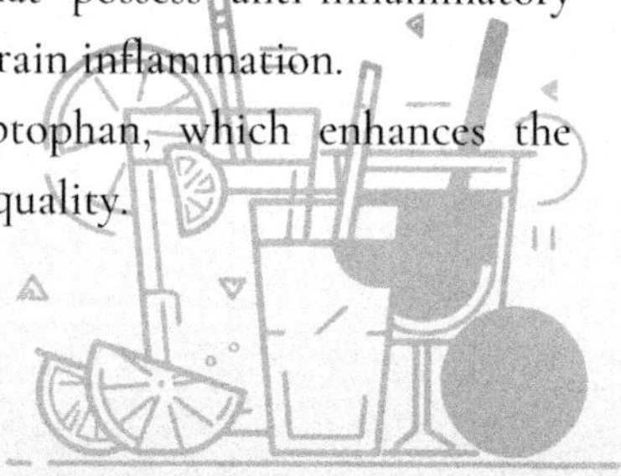

- **Ginger**: Ginger, apart from gingerol, contains a variety of potent anti-inflammatory and antioxidant compounds, which can mitigate factors that interfere with mood regulation.
- **Turmeric**: Curcumin, the main element in turmeric, is well-known for its anti-inflammatory and antioxidant qualities. Its potential role in elevating mood by increasing brain-derived neurotrophic factor (BDNF) is gaining attention.
- **Avocado**: This creamy fruit is a source of monounsaturated fats and tryptophan, promoting serotonin production. Plus, its B vitamins play a role in neurotransmitter synthesis, influencing mood and stress levels.
- **Kiwi**: Packed with vitamin C, kiwi may help manage the body's response to stress and counteract the damaging effects of oxidative stress on mood.
- Cacao or Dark Chocolate: Often used in smoothies, cacao is a reservoir of polyphenols that can improve mood and combat feelings of depression. Theobromine in cacao acts as a mild stimulant, lifting spirits.

Remember, while these ingredients have properties that can boost mood, consuming them as part of a balanced diet and maintaining a holistic approach to mental well-being is essential. The synergy of nutrition, physical activity, adequate sleep, and mindfulness practices can work wonders in ensuring consistent mood elevation.

Understanding Macronutrients and Micronutrients in Juices

Juicing can be a beautiful orchestra of nutrients when done right. Let's break down the basics of the essential nutrients present in the juices and understand their role.

Macronutrients: The Major Fuel Sources

Carbohydrates:

- ·What are they? They are our primary energy source. They break down into simpler sugars, providing immediate fuel.
- ·In Juices: Fruits are rich in natural sugars. When you juice an apple or an orange, you're primarily extracting its carbohydrates along with vitamins.
- ·Balancing Act: While fruits provide energy, veggies in juices, like celery or spinach, can help stabilize the sugar spike, offering a balanced energy release.

Proteins:

- ·What are they? Proteins are the building blocks. They help in repair, muscle-building, and overall growth.
- ·In Juices: Though juices aren't known for protein, some vegetables like kale and spinach have trace amounts. Incorporate seeds like chia or hemp to enhance protein content in your drink.

Fats:

- ·What are they? They support cellular function, brain health, and hormone production.
- In Juices: Not typically found in most fruit and vegetable juices. However, adding ingredients like avocado or flaxseeds can introduce healthy fats into your juice.

Macronutrients: The Major Fuel Sources

Vitamins:

- ·Why Important? They're crucial for energy production, immune function, and blood clotting, among other functions.
- ·In Juices: Different fruits and veggies offer different vitamins. For instance, citrus fruits are packed with Vitamin C, while carrots and sweet potatoes are rich in Vitamin A.

Minerals:

- ·Why Important? Minerals play roles in nerve signaling, muscle function, and bone-building.
- ·In Juices: Spinach and kale are rich in iron and calcium, while celery can be a good source of potassium.

Antioxidants:

- ·Why Important? They help combat free radicals in the body, which can cause cellular damage.
- ·In Juices: Berries, especially blueberries and strawberries, are rich in antioxidants. Even beetroot and pomegranate have substantial antioxidant properties.

Phytochemicals:

- ·Why Important? These are naturally occurring compounds in plants that have health benefits.
- ·In Juices: Cruciferous vegetables like broccoli and cabbage contain glucosinolates, and tomatoes are a good source of lycopene, both of which have potential anti-cancer properties.

In Summary, Juicing provides a concentrated dose of various nutrients. By understanding the roles of macronutrients and micronutrients, you can craft juices that cater specifically to your health needs.

Remember, the true power of juicing comes from the synergistic blend of nutrients, so aim for variety in your juices to harness the maximum benefits.

The Easy Method: Incorporating Juices Daily

Adding juices to your daily routine doesn't mean you have to give up that extra hour of sleep or sacrifice precious time. With the right strategy, juices can seamlessly fit into your life, irrespective of your schedule. Let's delve deeper into morning routines and tips for those who are always on the move.

Morning Rituals

Starting the day right can set the tone for everything that follows. Morning rituals, whether a series of stretches, a quiet moment of meditation, or a brisk walk, often determine our mood, energy levels, and outlook for the day. Incorporating a rejuvenating juice ritual into your morning can be a refreshing way to welcome the day, ensuring both body and mind are in harmony.

Wake-up Boosts: Energizing Morning Blends

- **Purpose**: Rise and shine takes on a whole new meaning with juices designed to awaken every cell in your body. These blends aim to kick-start metabolism, energize the mind, and invigorate the spirit.
- **Details**: Energizing ingredients typically include those high in vitamin C, antioxidants, and natural sugars. Think citrus fruits like oranges and grapefruits, complemented by the sweet undertones of ingredients like pineapples or apples.
- Blend Highlight: "Sunrise Zest" – A sunlit concoction of fresh orange, a slice of pineapple, and a dash of ginger. It's the liquid equivalent of a morning stretch, gently waking up the system and preparing it for the day ahead.
- Hydrating Starters: Setting the Tone for the Day
- Purpose: Before the caffeine kicks in or the breakfast sets on the plate, it's essential to hydrate. A hydrating starter ensures your body replenishes its overnight water loss, kick-starting every system from digestion to cognition.
- Details: Hydration heroes are often simple. Cucumbers, for instance, are over 90% water. Watermelon is another hydrating champion, offering not just moisture but also essential vitamins and minerals. Merging these with a splash of hydration-boosting coconut water can elevate their refreshing quotient.
- Blend Highlight: "Morning Dew Delight" – A refreshing medley of watermelon chunks, sliced cucumber, and a generous pour of coconut water. It's like a morning dew on the grass – cool, refreshing, and invigorating.
- As dawn breaks and a new day beckons, your morning juice ritual can be a cherished moment of solace, a sacred routine of self-care. With every sip, you're not just nourishing your body; you're also setting a positive, health-forward intention for the day. And with such a start, the day can only unfold beautifully, filled with energy, clarity, and joy.

For the Busy Bee

For those juggling tight schedules and seemingly endless tasks, the notion of incorporating a daily juice regimen might seem like another daunting commitment. However, with a touch of planning and a dash of enthusiasm, even the busiest among us can effortlessly imbibe the benefits of juicing. More than that, the entire process can be joyful and a moment of solace amidst the hustle.

Quick Combos for Nutritious On-the-Go Sips

- Purpose: Quick combos come to the rescue when you're pressed for time but your body is pressing for nutrition. They're not just easy and fast, but they bring a surge of vitality you can feel with every sip.
- Details: Think of ingredients that are easy to process. Bananas, for instance, can be peeled and tossed in. Berries are another quick add, with no prep needed. They're nature's fast food, offering an avalanche of antioxidants in seconds. Blend them with greens like spinach that require no chopping, and you have a nutrient-dense drink in minutes.
- Blend Highlight: "Burst of Busy Berry" – A delightful mixture of mixed berries, banana, spinach, and a spoonful of honey. It's sweet, it's nutritious, and best of all, it's swift.

Making Ahead: Storage and Preservation Tips

- ·Purpose: For those mornings when every second counts or those evenings when you foresee coming back exhausted, pre-made juices can be an elixir. The idea is to make it convenient without compromising the juice's essence.
- Details: It's all about the right storage to keep juices fresh and burst with nutrients. Use citrus bases like lemon to prevent oxidation. And, as an added tip, always use glass containers for storage. Not only do they keep the juice fresh, but they also prevent any contamination. Plus, there's something inherently satisfying about seeing your vibrant juice stored ready for consumption.
- Preservation Insight: When storing, keep it air-tight. It locks in freshness, ensures less oxidation, and promises a delightful taste even hours later.

Remember, the goal is to weave juicing into your life seamlessly. The happiness doesn't just come from the delightful flavors and the knowledge that, amidst all the busyness, you're taking a moment to prioritize yourself, nourish your body, and enjoy a slice of tranquility. With each gulp, there's a reminder that health and happiness can be simple and utterly delicious.

Evening Elixirs: Unwind & Recharge

The evening is not just about concluding your day; it's about preparing your body and mind for a restful night and a fresh start tomorrow. As the sun sets, our bodies transition from the bustling activities of the day to a state of relaxation and recovery. This phase is essential, as it's when our bodies repair, rejuvenate, and recharge. Tapping into the benefits of specific juices can play a pivotal role in enhancing this nightly rejuvenation.

Choosing the right ingredients for your evening juices is crucial. Ingredients rich in magnesium and potassium, like spinach and bananas, help in muscle relaxation, combating cramps, and restoring electrolyte balance. Antioxidants, found in abundance in berries and cherries, help in neutralizing the oxidative stress your body has encountered throughout the day.

Cherries stand out as an evening elixir champion due to their natural melatonin content, a hormone responsible for regulating sleep. A cherry-based juice blend can not only satisfy your taste buds but also guide you towards a restful sleep. Similarly, herbs like chamomile and lavender, known for their calming effects, can be incorporated into your juices to amplify relaxation.

Hydration remains a key aspect of evening juicing. Opt for ingredients with high water content, like cucumbers or watermelon, ensuring you're hydrated through the night without feeling overly full or bloated. Remember, the goal is to complement your dinner, not replace it.

Lastly, while the allure of fruits is undeniable, consider adding a hint of warmth with ingredients like ginger or turmeric. These not only boost your metabolism but also offer anti-inflammatory benefits, ensuring you wake up feeling refreshed and pain-free.

Incorporate these evening elixirs into your routine, and witness a transformation in your nighttime rituals, sleep quality, and overall well-being. Cheers to a calm evening and a brighter tomorrow!

Essential Juice Recipes
Detox and Cleanse Juices

These elixirs are crafted to support the body in eliminating toxins and resetting the digestive system. Detox juices focus on purifying the body with nutrient-rich ingredients that boost liver function and provide essential vitamins and antioxidants. Cleanse juices, often used in broader juice cleanse regimens, aim to give the digestive system a break from potential irritants like processed foods and sugars. Ingredients such as beets, leafy greens, celery, cucumber, and ginger are commonly found in these blends for their combined benefits of purification, hydration, and soothing properties. Whether seeking rejuvenation, energy, or a dietary reset, these juices offer a refreshing path to holistic well-being.

Purity Punch: Pineapple, Ginger, and Kale Symphony

Equipment

2 servings | 12 mins | 2 mins

Juicer, Knife, Cutting board

Ingredients

- Half of a medium-sized pineapple, peeled and cored
- 2-inch piece of fresh ginger root
- 4 large kale leaves
- 1 lemon, peeled (optional for extra zest)

Nutritional information:
135 calories; 3g protein; 32g carbohydrates; 0.6g fat; 3g fiber; 0mg cholesterol; 25mg sodium; 495mg potassium.

Directions

1. Start by washing the kale leaves thoroughly to remove any dirt or pesticides.
2. Peel the pineapple and ginger. If you're using lemon, ensure it's peeled to avoid a bitter taste.
3. Chop the pineapple, ginger, and kale into sizes that are suitable for your juicer.
4. Begin juicing with the kale leaves, as juicing the wetter pineapple afterward will help push through any kale remnants left in the juicer.
5. Follow with the ginger and then the pineapple. If using, finish with the lemon.
6. Give the juice a good stir, combine all flavors, and pour into glasses.
7. Consume immediately to enjoy the full nutritional benefits.

Benefits: The Purity Punch is a harmonious blend of zesty pineapple, spicy ginger, and earthy kale. Pineapple is high in Vitamin C and also contains bromelain, an enzyme that aids digestion. Ginger has been long celebrated for its anti-inflammatory and gastrointestinal benefits. Kale, being a superfood, is loaded with Vitamins A, K, and C and several antioxidants and minerals. This trio creates a rejuvenating and purifying blend, great for digestion, detoxification, and overall vitality.

Mellow Mender: Melon, Grapefruit, and Basil Blend

Equipment

Juicer or high-speed blender,
Strainer (if using a blender)

Ingredients

- 2 cups of fresh melon chunks (honeydew or cantaloupe)
- 1 large grapefruit, peeled and segmented
- A handful of fresh basil leaves

Nutritional information:
120 calories; 1.5g protein; 30g carbohydrates; 0.3g fat; 2g fiber; 0mg cholesterol; 15mg sodium; 410mg potassium.

2 servings | 16 mins | 0 mins

Directions

1. Start by washing and preparing all the ingredients.
2. If using a juicer, start with the melon chunks, followed by the grapefruit segments, and finish with the basil leaves.
3. If using a blender, combine all the ingredients and blend until smooth. If preferred, strain the mixture to eliminate any pulp or basil fragments.
4. Pour the juice into glasses and serve right away. Consider garnishing with a small melon ball or an extra basil leaf for a picturesque finish.
5. Revel in the soothing and refreshing flavors that Mellow Mender offers.
6. If not used right away, store the blend in an airtight jar in the refrigerator for up to 24 hours.
7. Give it a quick stir or shake before consuming if stored.

***Benefits**: Mellow Mender is a harmonious blend of sweet melon, tangy grapefruit, and aromatic basil. Melons are a hydrating fruit rich in vitamins and minerals that promote skin health and hydration. Grapefruit, known for its immune-boosting vitamin C, also aids in digestion and may help in weight management. The addition of basil brings a touch of freshness and is rich in antioxidants and anti-inflammatory properties, making this blend both delicious and therapeutic*

Toxin Terminator: Tangerine, Beetroot, and Spinach Splendor

Equipment

Juicer or high-speed blender, Strainer (if using a blender)

Ingredients

- 3 medium-sized tangerines, peeled and segmented
- 2 medium beetroots, washed, peeled, and chopped
- 2 cups fresh spinach leaves, cleaned and roughly sliced

Nutritional information:
95 calories; 2.8g protein; 22g carbohydrates; 0.5g fat; 3.5g fiber; 0mg cholesterol; 80mg sodium; 520mg potassium.

3 servings 19 mins 0 mins

Directions

1. Thoroughly wash and prepare all the ingredients.
2. If using a juicer, begin with the tangerine segments, followed by beetroot pieces, and conclude with the spinach leaves.
3. If you're using a blender, combine all of the ingredients and blend until smooth. If desired, strain the blend to discard any pulp.
4. Transfer the juice to glasses and serve immediately for a fresh experience. A slice of tangerine or a spinach leaf can serve as an appealing garnish.
5. Savor the rich and refreshing taste of the Toxin Terminator blend.
6. If not consumed right away, make sure the juice is stored in a sealed container in the refrigerator, ideally not for more than 24 hours.
7. Prior to drinking from storage, give the blend a brief stir or shake.

***Benefits**: The Toxin Terminator blend is a power-packed combination designed to cleanse and rejuvenate your body. Tangerines are not only sweet and juicy, but they are also high in vitamin C, which aids in immunity and promotes healthy skin. Beetroot, a superfood, is packed with vitamins, minerals, and potent antioxidants that support liver detoxification, boost stamina, and can help lower blood pressure. Spinach, on the other hand, is a leafy green powerhouse filled with iron, calcium, and magnesium, aiding in energy production, bone health, and muscle function.*

Glowing Gusher: Green Apple, Fennel, and Aloe Vera Alliance

2 servings | 16 mins | 0 mins

Equipment

Juicer, high-speed blender, strainer (for those using a blender), knife.

Ingredients

- 2 large green apples, cored and sliced
- 1 medium-sized fennel bulb, washed and sliced
- 3 tablespoons of pure aloe vera gel (ensure it's edible and free from additives)

Nutritional information:
110 calories; 1.5g protein; 26g carbohydrates; 0.3g fat; 4g fiber; 0mg cholesterol; 50mg sodium; 430mg potassium.

Directions

1. Prepare all ingredients by washing, coring, and slicing as necessary.
2. For juicers: Begin with the apple slices, followed by the fennel, and finally add the aloe vera gel.
3. For blenders: Combine all ingredients and blend until smooth. Use a strainer to remove any pulp, if desired.
4. Serve the fresh juice in glasses. A slice of apple or fennel can be used as garnish.
5. Relish the unique taste and feel the glow it brings.
6. If not drunk right away, store the juice in a sealed jar in the refrigerator. It remains fresh for up to 24 hours.
7. Prior to consumption from storage, give it a good stir or shake.

***Benefits**: The Glowing Gusher blend is meticulously crafted to enhance your skin's radiance and maintain internal hydration. Green apples are laden with antioxidants that combat skin aging. Fennel's anti-inflammatory properties can help in reducing skin irritations, while aloe vera provides deep hydration and accelerates skin repair.*

Purge Powerhouse: Pear, Arugula, and Lemon Liaison

Equipment

Juicer, high-speed blender, strainer (for those using a blender), knife.

Ingredients

- 2 medium ripe pears, cored and sliced
- 2 cups of fresh arugula leaves, washed
- Juice of 1 lemon

Nutritional information:
95 calories; 1g protein; 24g carbohydrates; 0.2g fat; 5g fiber; 0mg cholesterol; 10mg sodium; 230mg potassium.

2 servings | 10 mins | 0 mins

Directions

1. Thoroughly wash, core, and slice the pears. Prepare the arugula leaves by washing them.
2. For juicers: Start with pear slices, followed by arugula. Lastly, add the freshly squeezed lemon juice to the mix.
3. For blenders: Add all ingredients to the blender and blend until smooth. Use a strainer for a pulp-free juice, if preferred.
4. Pour out the juice into glasses and serve immediately. Garnishing with a pear slice or a lemon wedge can elevate its presentation.
5. Delight in the zesty and refreshing flavors of the Purge Powerhouse blend.
6. Should there be leftovers, transfer to a sealed container and refrigerate. Consume within 24 hours for optimal freshness.
7. Remember to shake or stir well before consumption if taken from storage.

***Benefits**: The Glowing Gusher blend is meticulously crafted to enhance your skin's radiance and maintain internal hydration. Green apples are laden with antioxidants that combat skin aging. Fennel's anti-inflammatory properties can help in reducing skin irritations, while aloe vera provides deep hydration and accelerates skin repair.*

Vitality Vortex: Carrot, Turmeric, and Lime Leap

Equipment

2 servings 15 mins 0 mins

Juicer, high-speed blender, strainer (for those using a blender), knife.

Ingredients

- 4 medium-sized carrots, washed and peeled
- 1-inch piece of fresh turmeric root, washed (or 1 teaspoon of turmeric powder)
- Juice of 2 limes

Nutritional information:
70 calories; 1.2g protein; 16g carbohydrates; 0.4g fat; 4g fiber; 0mg cholesterol; 70mg sodium; 390mg potassium.

Directions

1. Prepare carrots by washing, peeling, and cutting them into manageable pieces. Clean the turmeric root.
2. For juicers: Begin with carrot pieces, add the turmeric, and end with freshly squeezed lime juice.
3. For blenders: Combine carrots, turmeric, and lime juice, then blend until smooth. Strain to remove pulp, if desired.
4. Serve the vibrant juice in glasses. A slice of lime or a sprinkle of turmeric can be added as a garnish for a more appealing look.
5. Revel in the invigorating and zestful taste of the Vitality Vortex blend.
6. If not consumed immediately, store the juice in a sealed container in the refrigerator. It's best consumed within 24 hours for peak freshness.
7. Always shake or stir the blend before consumption if retrieved from storage.

***Benefits**: The Vitality Vortex blend is a delightful burst of energy and nutrients in a glass. Carrots, high in beta-carotene, improve eye health and supply important vitamins and antioxidants. Turmeric, with its active compound curcumin, offers potent anti-inflammatory benefits and may help ward off chronic diseases. Lime, packed with vitamin C, elevates the flavor profile and aids in digestion and skin health.*

Herbal Harmony: Celery, Parsley, and Kiwi Kombination

Equipment

2 servings 15 mins 0 mins

Juicer, high-speed blender, strainer (for those using a blender), knife.

Ingredients

- 4 celery stalks, washed and chopped
- A handful of fresh parsley, roughly chopped
- 2 ripe kiwis, peeled and sliced

Nutritional information:
85 calories; 2g protein; 20g carbohydrates; 0.3g fat; 4.5g fibre; 0mg cholesterol; 80mg sodium; 430mg potassium.

Directions

1. Wash and prepare all the ingredients by chopping and slicing.
2. For juicers: Start with the celery stalks, followed by parsley, and then the kiwi slices.
3. For blenders: Add all the ingredients and blend until a smooth consistency is achieved. You can strain the juice to remove pulp, if preferred.
4. Pour the verdant juice into glasses. Garnishing with a slice of kiwi or a parsley leaf adds to its aesthetic appeal.
5. Savor the refreshingly herbal and tangy flavors of the Herbal Harmony blend.
6. If not consumed immediately, store the juice in a sealed container in the fridge and aim to consume within 24 hours.
7. Prior to drinking from storage, ensure to give it a good stir or shake.

***Benefits**: The Herbal Harmony blend marries the refreshing crispness of celery with the herbal kick of parsley, topped off with the tangy sweetness of kiwi. Celery hydrates and provides a good dose of fiber, aiding digestion. Parsley is abundant in vitamin K, crucial for bone health. Kiwi stands out not just for its unique taste but also its impressive vitamin C content, boosting skin health and immunity*

Soothing Sipper: Strawberry, Cilantro, and Ginger Grace

Equipment

2 servings | 10 mins | 0 mins

Juicer, high-speed blender, strainer (for those using a blender), knife.

Ingredients

- 1 cup of strawberries, hulled and halved
- A handful of fresh cilantro washed and roughly chopped
- 1 inch fresh ginger, peeled and sliced

Nutritional information:
60 calories; 1.2g protein; 14g carbohydrates; 0.3g fat; 3g fiber; 0mg cholesterol; 5mg sodium; 230mg potassium.

Directions

1. Wash and prepare all ingredients.
2. For juicers: Begin with strawberries, then add the cilantro, and finally, the ginger slices.
3. For blenders: Add strawberries, cilantro, and ginger into the blender and blend until smooth. If you want a smoother consistency, filter the juice to remove the pulp.
4. Serve the aromatic juice in glasses. Garnish with a strawberry half or a sprig of cilantro for an appealing touch.
5. Relish the delightful amalgamation of sweet, herbal, and spicy notes in the Soothing Sipper blend.
6. If not consumed immediately, transfer the juice to a sealed container and refrigerate. It's best consumed within 24 hours to ensure freshness.
7. If taken from storage, ensure to shake or stir well before serving.

***Benefits**: Dive into a symphony of flavors with the Soothing Sipper blend. Strawberries, with their high vitamin C and antioxidant content, rejuvenate the skin and boost the immune system. Cilantro is renowned for its detoxifying properties and is believed to help remove heavy metals from the body. Ginger adds a zing to the mix and is celebrated for its anti-inflammatory and digestive-aiding properties*

Rejuvenation Rush: Raspberry, Orange, and Dandelion Dream

Equipment

Juicer, high-speed blender, strainer (for those using a blender), knife.

2 servings | 15 mins | 0 mins

Ingredients

- 1 cup of fresh raspberries
- 2 oranges, peeled and segmented
- A handful of dandelion greens, washed and roughly chopped

Nutritional information:
90 calories; 2g protein; 22g carbohydrates; 0.4g fat; 5g fiber; 0mg cholesterol; 10mg sodium; 300mg potassium.

Directions

1. Prepare the ingredients by washing, peeling, chopping, and segmenting as required.
2. For juicers: Start with the raspberries, add the orange segments, and finish with the dandelion greens.
3. For blenders: Place raspberries, orange segments, and dandelion greens into the blender and process until smooth. If a finer consistency is desired, strain the juice to remove any pulp.
4. Pour the bright-hued juice into glasses. A raspberry or an orange slice can serve as a lovely garnish.
5. Dive into the zesty, sweet, and slightly bitter medley of flavors that the Rejuvenation Rush offers.
6. If any juice remains, store it in a sealed container in the refrigerator. To ensure optimal taste and nutrition, consume within 24 hours.
7. Remember to shake or stir the juice well if drinking from storage.

***Benefits**: Immerse yourself in a vibrant blend designed to rejuvenate from the inside out. Raspberries, rich in antioxidants and vitamins, provide a burst of refreshing tartness. Oranges, packed with vitamin C, enhance skin quality and bolster the immune system. Dandelion, often underrated, acts as a detoxifier for the liver and is a great source of various minerals and vitamins*

Refresh Radiance: Cherry, Kale, and Mint Mix

2 servings | 15 mins | 0 mins

Equipment

Juicer, high-speed blender, strainer (if using a blender), knife.

Ingredients

- 1 cup of fresh cherries, pitted
- 2 cups of kale, washed and roughly chopped
- A handful of fresh mint leaves

Nutritional information:
80 calories; 2.5g protein; 18g carbohydrates; 0.5g fat; 3.5g fiber; 0mg cholesterol; 30mg sodium; 420mg potassium.

Directions

1. Prepare the ingredients by washing, pitting, and chopping as necessary.
2. For juicers: Begin with the cherries, followed by the kale, and then add the mint leaves for that final refreshing touch.
3. For blenders: Combine cherries, kale, and mint leaves in the blender and blend until you achieve a smooth consistency. If you prefer a more refined texture, strain the juice to separate the pulp.
4. Serve this rich-colored juice in glasses. A sprig of mint or a cherry can enhance its presentation.
5. Enjoy the sweet and tangy notes complemented by the cool undertone of mint in the Refresh Radiance blend.
6. For any leftovers, transfer to a sealed container and refrigerate. It's recommended to consume within 24 hours to retain its freshness and nutrient value.
7. If consuming from storage, make sure to give it a good stir or shake before enjoying it.

***Benefits**: Indulge in a delightful burst of nutrition and flavor with the Refresh Radiance blend. Cherries, packed with antioxidants and anti-inflammatory compounds, promote heart health and can improve sleep quality. Kale, often dubbed the "queen of greens," is nutrient-dense, providing a host of vitamins and minerals. Mint not only adds a refreshing kick but also aids digestion and imparts a cooling effect.*

Detox Duet: Watermelon and Rosemary Rhapsody

Equipment

Juicer, high-speed blender, strainer (for those using a blender), knife.

Ingredients

- 4 cups watermelon cubes, seeds removed
- 2 sprigs fresh rosemary, leaves stripped

Nutritional information: 60 calories; 1g protein; 15g carbohydrates; 0.3g fat; 0.9g fiber; 0mg cholesterol; 2mg sodium; 210mg potassium.

2 servings | 12 mins | 0 mins

Directions

1. Start by prepping your watermelon. Remove the peel and seeds, then cut the flesh into cubes.
2. Wash the rosemary sprigs thoroughly.
3. Place the watermelon cubes into the juicer, followed by the rosemary.
4. Juice until you've extracted as much liquid as possible.
5. Pour out into serving glasses, stir well, and enjoy immediately for the best flavor and nutrient retention.

***Benefits**: Hydrate and invigorate with this refreshing mix. Watermelon aids in hydration, while rosemary provides an aromatic touch that is believed to enhance memory and concentration.*

Clear Clarity: Cabbage, Blueberry, and Lime Lullaby

2 servings | 12 mins | 0 mins

Equipment

Juicer, high-speed blender, strainer (for those using a blender), knife.

Ingredients

- 1 cup chopped cabbage
- 1 cup blueberries
- Juice of 1 lime

Nutritional information:
85 calories; 2g protein; 20g carbohydrates; 0.5g fat; 4g fiber; 0mg cholesterol; 25mg sodium; 250mg potassium.

Directions

1. Prepare the cabbage by washing it and chopping it into manageable pieces.
2. Rinse the blueberries to ensure they're clean and free from any debris.
3. Obtain the lime's juice using a manual juicer or by squeezing the fruit.
4. Place the chopped cabbage and blueberries into the juicer.
5. Once juiced, add the lime juice, stir well.
6. Serve in a chilled glass for an invigorating experience.
7.

***Benefits**: Cabbage promotes gut health, blueberries are antioxidant powerhouses, and lime adds a vitamin C boost.*

Green Guardian: Spinach, Cucumber, and Green Apple Gala

2 servings 12 mins 0 mins

Equipment

Juicer, high-speed blender, strainer (for those using a blender), knife.

Ingredients

- 2 cups fresh spinach
- 1 cucumber, sliced
- 1 green apple, cored and sliced

Nutritional information:
95 calories; 2.5g protein; 22g carbohydrates; 0.4g fat; 4.8g fiber; 0mg cholesterol; 35mg sodium; 320mg potassium.

Directions

1. Thoroughly wash the spinach leaves, cucumber, and green apple.
2. Core and slice the green apple into thin wedges.
3. Slice the cucumber into manageable pieces.
4. Start by juicing the spinach leaves, followed by the cucumber slices.
5. Add the green apple wedges last.
6. Stir the combined juice for an even blend.
7. Pour into glasses and serve immediately.

Benefits: *A powerful blend of vitamins and minerals. Spinach provides iron, cucumber hydrates, and apple adds dietary fiber.*

Body Balance: Banana, Chia Seed, and Lemon Loop

Equipment

2 servings | 10 mins | 0 mins

Blender, knife

Directions

1. Peel and slice the bananas into chunks.
2. In a blender, combine the banana chunks and lemon juice.
3. Blend until smooth and creamy.
4. Add the chia seeds and pulse briefly so that they are equitably distributed.
5. Let the blend sit for 2-3 minutes allowing the chia seeds to absorb some liquid.
6. Pour out into glasses, garnish with a lemon slice if desired, and serve.

Ingredients

- 2 bananas
- 2 tbsp chia seeds
- Juice of 1 lemon

Nutritional information:
190 calories; 3g protein; 40g carbohydrates; 3g fat; 6g fiber; 0mg cholesterol; 5mg sodium; 420mg potassium.

***Benefits**: A mix to stabilize energy levels. Banana provides potassium, chia seeds offer fiber and omega-3s, and lemon provides vitamin C.*

Pure Passion: Passionfruit, Ginger, and Broccoli Burst

3 servings | 15 mins | 0 mins

Equipment

Blender, Knife, Strainer, Measuring cups, Serving glass

Ingredients

- 3 ripe passionfruits, halved
- 1 inch of fresh ginger, trimmed and sliced
- 1 cup of broccoli florets

Nutritional information:
90 calories; 2g protein; 20g carbohydrates; 0.5g fat; 6g fiber; 0mg cholesterol; 25mg sodium; 370mg potassium.

Directions

1. Scoop out the passionfruit pulp and place it in the blender.
2. Add the sliced ginger.
3. Steam broccoli florets until they're soft enough to blend. Allow them to cool and add them to the blender.
4. Blend at high speed until all ingredients are thoroughly combined.
5. Use a strainer to sieve the juice, discarding the seeds and any large pieces.
6. Pour out the strained juice into glasses and enjoy immediately.

***Benefits**: Venture into a blend where passion meets zest! Passionfruit, the core of this recipe, is a treasure trove of vitamin C and dietary fiber, promoting skin health and digestive well-being. Ginger adds a spicy undertone and aids in inflammation reduction, while broccoli, the unsung hero, provides essential vitamins and minerals for overall health. This drink is a symphony of flavors and wellness.*

Lively Lifter: Lychee, Beet, and Celery Cadenza

Equipment

Juicer, blender, knife

2 servings | 15 mins | 0 mins

Directions

1. Begin by ensuring the lychees are peeled, and the stones are removed. Chop the beet and celery into manageable pieces.
2. Using a juicer, process the lychees first, followed by the beet and celery. If you're using a blender, combine all ingredients and blend until smooth. Straining the juice after blending will provide a clearer consistency.
3. Pour the resulting blend into glasses. For an added touch, garnish with a small celery stick or lychee.
4. Immerse yourself in the unique and energizing flavors of the Lively Lifter blend!

Ingredients

- 10 fresh lychees, peeled and pitted
- 1 medium-sized beet, peeled and chopped
- 2 celery stalks, thoroughly washed and chopped

Nutritional information:
110 calories; 2.5g protein; 26g carbohydrates; 0.3g fat; 3.5g fiber; 0mg cholesterol; 60mg sodium; 350mg potassium.

Benefits: *Dive into a blend that's a true energy booster! Lychee is laden with vitamin C, ensuring a radiant skin glow. Beets are well-known for enhancing athletic performance and increasing blood flow, while celery adds a hydration kick with its high water content and beneficial salts.*

Flush Fusion: Figs, Pineapple, and Lemon Balm Fusion

Equipment

Juicer, blender, knife

2 servings | 10 mins | 0 mins

Directions

1. If using a juicer, process figs, pineapple, and lemon balm leaves through the machine. If you're using a blender, combine all ingredients and blend until smooth. For a finer consistency, consider straining the juice after blending.
2. Pour into glasses and consider garnishing with a small sprig of lemon balm for visual appeal.
3. Revel in the soothing and refreshing taste of the Flush Fusion blend.

Ingredients

- 6 fresh figs, stemmed and halved
- 1 cup fresh pineapple chunks
- A handful of fresh lemon balm leaves, washed

Nutritional information:
130 calories; 2g protein; 32g carbohydrates; 0.5g fat; 5.5g fiber; 0mg cholesterol; 15mg sodium; 340mg potassium

***Benefits**: Embark on a journey of internal cleansing with this blend. Figs, rich in dietary fiber, promote digestive health. Pineapple, containing the enzyme bromelain, aids in protein digestion. The calming properties of lemon balm can alleviate stress and soothe the digestive tract.*

Svelte Symphony: Blackberry, Lemon, and Jalapeno Jive

2 servings | 10 mins | 0 mins

Equipment

Juicer, blender, knife

Ingredients

- 1 cup fresh blackberries
- Juice of 1 lemon
- 1 small jalapeno, seeds removed (adjust based on heat preference)

Nutritional information:
70 calories; 1.5g protein; 17g carbohydrates; 0.6g fat; 4g fiber; 0mg cholesterol; 5mg sodium; 230mg potassium

Directions

1. Prepare your ingredients by washing the blackberries, juicing the lemon, and deseeding the jalapeno. For milder heat, ensure all seeds and membranes are removed from the jalapeno.
2. If using a juicer, process blackberries, followed by adding the lemon juice and jalapeno. If you're using a blender, combine all ingredients and blend until smooth. For a silkier consistency, consider straining the juice after blending.
3. Pour your vibrant blend into glasses and, if you wish, garnish with a blackberry or a thin slice of jalapeno for an adventurous touch.
4. Savor the invigorating flavors of the Svelte Symphony, and feel the zesty jive!

***Benefits**: Dance to the rhythm of a metabolic boost with this spicy and tangy concoction. Blackberries, loaded with fiber and vitamins, promote digestive health. Lemon's alkalizing properties aid in balancing the body's pH, while the kick of jalapeno, thanks to its capsaicin content, can enhance metabolism and promote fat burning.*

Crystal Cascade: Cranberry, Cilantro, and Orange Odyssey

Equipment

Juicer, blender, knife

Ingredients

- 1 cup fresh cranberries
- 1 handful of cilantro, washed and roughly chopped
- Juice of 2 oranges

Nutritional information:
90 calories; 1g protein; 22g carbohydrates; 0.3g fat; 3.5g fiber; 0mg cholesterol; 10mg sodium; 250mg potassium.

2 servings | 12 mins | 0 mins

Directions

1. Begin by washing the cranberries and cilantro thoroughly. Juice the oranges, either manually or with an electronic juicer.
2. If using a juicer, start with cranberries, followed by cilantro, and then add the orange juice. If you're using a blender, combine all ingredients and blend until smooth. Consider straining the juice after blending for a smoother texture.
3. Pour the vibrant red blend into glasses. For an aesthetic touch, garnish with an orange slice or a sprig of cilantro.
4. Immerse yourself in the refreshing and tangy flavors of the Crystal Cascade.

Benefits: *With a cascade of antioxidants and refreshing flavors, this blend is your ticket to vitality. Cranberries are renowned for their UTI-prevention properties and high antioxidant content. Cilantro is believed to assist in heavy metal detoxification. The burst of orange adds a dose of vitamin C, further enhancing the detox process and boosting your immunity.*

Radiant Rhythm: Red Grape, Watercress, and Cucumber Concerto

Equipment

Juicer, blender, knife

2 servings | 12 mins | 0 mins

Directions

1. Thoroughly wash all ingredients. If desired, peel the cucumber for a milder flavor.
2. If using a juicer, process grapes first, followed by watercress and cucumber. If you're using a blender, combine all ingredients and blend until smooth. Straining the juice after blending can provide a more refined texture.
3. Pour the luminous green blend into glasses. As a garnishing touch, float a few grapes on top or add a slice of cucumber to the rim.
4. Dive into the crisp, refreshing flavors of the Radiant Rhythm.

Ingredients

- 1 cup red grapes
- 1 handful of watercress, washed
- 1 medium cucumber, sliced

Nutritional information:
80 calories; 2g protein; 20g carbohydrates; 0.2g fat; 2g fiber; 0mg cholesterol; 15mg sodium; 320mg potassium.

***Benefits**: A melody of hydration and antioxidants, this blend promotes glowing skin and improved circulation. Red grapes, packed with resveratrol, offer anti-inflammatory benefits. Watercress, a peppery supergreen, provides a wealth of vitamins and minerals, while cucumber offers hydration and skin-soothing properties.*

Weight Management Juices

Dive into the world of Weight Management Juices, where each sip is tailored to support your weight goals. This chapter explores blends designed to balance nourishment and calorie-consciousness. Unearth recipes that not only invigorate metabolism but also curb cravings, acting as perfect allies in your weight management endeavors. From the verdant greens to the zesty citruses, discover how these natural ingredients can pave a flavorful path to a healthier you.

Lean Lush: Grapefruit, Kale, and Cayenne Combo

Equipment

2 servings | 12 mins | 0 mins

Blender, knife, cutting board

Ingredients

- 1 large grapefruit, peeled and seeded
- 1 cup of kale leaves, washed
- A pinch of cayenne pepper

Nutritional information:
110 calories; 2.5g protein; 25g carbohydrates; 1g fat; 5g fiber; 0mg cholesterol; 20mg sodium; 300mg potassium.

Directions

1. Prepare the grapefruit by peeling and ensuring all seeds are removed.
2. Add grapefruit pieces, kale leaves, and cayenne pepper to the blender.
3. Blend until smooth.
4. Serve immediately in chilled glasses.

Benefits: *The "Lean Lush" mixture is a metabolic booster. Grapefruit is a well-known catalyst for weight management and fat burning. Kale, low in calories but dense in nutrients, gives the body what it needs without the weight gain. A hint of cayenne pepper further revs up the metabolism, making this drink a weight-loss powerhouse.*

Metabolic Majesty: Pineapple, Celery, and Turmeric Twist

Equipment

Blender, knife, cutting board

2 servings | 14 mins | 0 mins

Directions

1. Prepare the pineapple and celery.
2. Combine pineapple chunks, chopped celery, and turmeric powder in a blender.
3. Blend until you achieve a velvety texture.
4. Pour into glasses and serve chilled.

Ingredients

- 1 cup pineapple chunks
- 2 celery stalks, washed and chopped
- ½ teaspoon turmeric powder

Nutritional information:
95 calories; 1.5g protein; 23g carbohydrates; 0.5g fat; 4g fiber; 0mg cholesterol; 25mg sodium; 280mg potassium.

***Benefits**: Boost your metabolism with the "Metabolic Majesty". Pineapples are rich in bromelain, aiding digestion. Celery provides dietary fiber that promotes gut health and weight management. Turmeric, a golden spice, not only lends a unique flavor but also contains curcumin known for its anti-inflammatory benefits and boosting metabolism.*

Fat-Fighter Fusion: Blackberry, Cucumber, and Lemon Liaison

Equipment

Blender, knife, cutting board.

Ingredients

- 1 cup blackberries
- 1 cucumber, sliced
- Juice of 1 lemon

Nutritional information:
95 calories; 1.5g protein; 23g carbohydrates; 0.5g fat; 4g fiber; 0mg cholesterol; 25mg sodium; 280mg potassium.

2 servings 10 mins 0 mins

Directions

1. Prepare the ingredients: wash blackberries, slice cucumber, and extract lemon juice.
2. Place all the ingredients in the blender.
3. Blend until smooth and silky.
4. Serve immediately for a refreshing treat.

***Benefits**: A refreshing blend designed to fight fat. Blackberries are high in antioxidants, which help to reduce fat storage. Cucumber, with its hydrating properties, aids in flushing out toxins, while lemon provides vitamin C and boosts digestion.*

Trim Tonic: Pomegranate, Beetroot, and Mint Marvel

2 servings | 15 mins | 0 mins

Equipment

Blender, knife, cutting board.

Ingredients

- 1 cup pomegranate seeds
- 1 small beetroot, peeled and chopped
- A handful of mint leaves

Nutritional information:
115 calories; 2.5g protein; 26g carbohydrates; 1g fat; 6g fiber; 0mg cholesterol; 30mg sodium; 310mg potassium.

Directions

1. Prepare the pomegranate seeds, chop the beetroot, and wash the mint leaves.
2. Combine all the ingredients in the blender.
3. Blend until you achieve a luscious texture.
4. Serve it cold with a sprig of mint on top.

***Benefits**: The "Trim Tonic" offers a mix of flavors and potent weight management benefits. Pomegranates are rich in antioxidants, beetroots help in detoxifying, and mint aids digestion. This combination ensures you not only relish the taste but also reap weight management benefits*

Waistline Whisperer: Watermelon, Chia Seed, and Lime Link-up

Equipment

Blender, knife, cutting board.

2 servings | 10 mins | 0 mins

Directions

1. Cube the watermelon and set aside.
2. In a blender, combine watermelon chunks, chia seeds, and lime juice.
3. Blend until smooth.
4. Serve immediately for the best flavor.

Ingredients

- 2 cups watermelon chunks
- 2 tablespoons chia seeds
- Juice of 1 lime

Nutritional information:
105 calories; 3g protein; 24g carbohydrates; 2g fat; 4g fiber; 0mg cholesterol; 10mg sodium; 295mg potassium.

***Benefits**: This delightful concoction provides a hydrating and refreshing taste. Watermelon aids in hydration, chia seeds offer fiber and protein to help keep you full, and lime gives a zesty boost of vitamin C. This blend supports a reduced calorie intake and a healthy metabolic rate*

Belly Buster Brew: Blueberry, Fennel, and Aloe Vera Alliance

Equipment

Blender, knife, cutting board.

2 servings | 15 mins | 0 mins

Ingredients

- 1 cup blueberries
- 1 medium fennel bulb, sliced
- 2 tablespoons aloe vera gel

Nutritional information:
115 calories; 2g protein; 26g carbohydrates; 0.5g fat; 6g fiber; 0mg cholesterol; 10mg sodium; 320mg potassium.

Directions

1. Wash blueberries and fennel thoroughly.
2. Combine blueberries, sliced fennel, and aloe vera gel in a blender.
3. Blend until smooth.
4. Pour and serve chilled.

***Benefits**: Loaded with antioxidants from blueberries, digestive aid from fennel, and the soothing properties of aloe vera, this juice can help in digestion, boost metabolism, and combat bloating.*

Svelte Smoothie: Strawberry, Basil, and Green Tea Grace

Equipment

2 servings 15 mins 0 mins

Blender, knife, cutting board.

Directions

1. Hull and halve the strawberries.
2. Make the green tea, then let it cool.
3. In a blender, combine strawberries, basil leaves, and cooled green tea.
4. Blend until smooth and serve immediately.

Ingredients

- 1 cup strawberries
- 6-8 fresh basil leaves
- 1 cup brewed green tea, cooled

Nutritional information:
70 calories; 1g protein; 16g carbohydrates; 0.5g fat; 3g fiber; 0mg cholesterol; 5mg sodium; 240mg potassium.

Benefits: *Strawberries offer a burst of vitamins and fiber, basil provides a refreshing twist with anti-inflammatory benefits, and green tea is renowned for its metabolism-boosting catechins. A perfect blend to support weight loss while pampering your taste buds*

Pound Plunge Potion: Kiwi, Arugula, and Ginger Gush

Equipment

Blender, knife, cutting board.

2 servings | 10 mins | 0 mins

Directions

1. Prepare kiwis by peeling and slicing them.
2. Roughly chop the ginger.
3. In a blender, combine kiwi slices, fresh arugula, and chopped ginger.
4. Blend until smooth and serve immediately.

Ingredients

- 3 ripe kiwis, peeled and sliced
- 2 cups fresh arugula
- 1-inch ginger piece, peeled

Nutritional information:
90 calories; 2g protein; 22g carbohydrates; 0.5g fat; 5g fiber; 0mg cholesterol; 10mg sodium; 420mg potassium.

Benefits: *Kiwi is a potent source of vitamin C and fiber, aiding in digestion and boosting metabolism. Arugula, packed with nitrates, helps in improving athletic performance. Ginger complements its anti-inflammatory properties and metabolism-boosting effects, making this blend a dynamic weight management ally.*

Lite Delight: Orange, Broccoli, and Spinach Symphony

Equipment

2 servings | 12 mins | 0 mins

Blender, knife, cutting board.

Ingredients

- 2 large oranges, peeled and segmented
- 1 cup broccoli florets
- 2 cups fresh spinach

Nutritional information:
95 calories; 4g protein; 23g carbohydrates; 0.5g fat; 6g fiber; 0mg cholesterol; 50mg sodium; 590mg potassium.

Directions

1. Prepare the oranges by peeling and segmenting them.
2. Wash broccoli florets and spinach leaves thoroughly.
3. In a blender, combine orange segments, broccoli, and spinach.
4. Blend until smooth and serve chilled.

***Benefits**: This juice blend promotes a robust immune system with the vitamin C from oranges, detoxifies with the aid of broccoli, and offers a rich iron content from spinach, which supports healthy metabolism. A fusion that not only aids weight management but also enhances overall well-being.*

Calorie Cutter: Cherry, Lemon, and Flaxseed Fantasy

Equipment

Blender, knife, cutting board.

2 servings 8 mins 0 mins

Directions

1. Remove pits from the cherries.
2. Squeeze juice from the lemon.
3. Combine cherries, lemon juice, and flaxseeds in a blender.
4. Blend until smooth and serve immediately.

Ingredients

- 1 cup cherries, pitted
- 1 lemon, juiced
- 2 tablespoons flaxseeds

Nutritional information:
105 calories; 3g protein; 25g carbohydrates; 3g fat; 6g fiber; 0mg cholesterol; 5mg sodium; 320mg potassium.

Benefits*: Cherries are not only delicious but are also known to speed up metabolism. The vitamin C from lemons aids in fat oxidation, while flaxseeds are packed with fiber that helps you feel full and satisfied, preventing overeating. This is the ultimate fat-burning and appetite-curbing potion.*

Fit & Fresh Fusion: Raspberry, Carrot, and Cilantro Concoction

Equipment

Blender, knife, cutting board.

Ingredients

- 1 cup raspberries
- 2 large carrots, peeled and sliced
- A handful of cilantro leaves

Nutritional information:
85 calories; 2g protein; 20g carbohydrates; 0.5g fat; 7g fiber; 0mg cholesterol; 45mg sodium; 410mg potassium.

2 servings | 10 mins | 0 mins

Directions

1. Wash raspberries thoroughly.
2. Prepare the carrots by peeling and slicing them.
3. In a blender, combine raspberries, carrot slices, and cilantro leaves.
4. Blend until smooth, then serve immediately.

***Benefits**: Raspberries are brimming with metabolism-boosting ketones. Carrots, rich in beta-carotene, support the health of your eyes and skin. Cilantro offers detoxifying properties, making this juice not only a treat for the taste buds but also a boost for your overall health.*

Weight Wane Wonder: Pear, Ginger, and Kale Kick

Equipment

2 servings | 10 mins | 0 mins

Blender, knife, cutting board.

Ingredients

- 2 ripe pears, cored and sliced
- 1-inch piece of ginger, peeled
- 2 cups of kale, stems removed

Nutritional information:
110 calories; 3g protein; 28g carbohydrates; 0.5g fat; 6g fiber; 0mg cholesterol; 30mg sodium; 450mg potassium.

Directions

1. Prepare the pears by coring and slicing them.
2. Peel the ginger and roughly chop.
3. Combine pears, ginger, and kale in a blender.
4. Blend until smooth and enjoy immediately.

***Benefits**: Pears, with their high fiber content, make you feel full and stabilize your blood sugar levels. Ginger boosts metabolism, aids digestion, and provides anti-inflammatory benefits. Kale, a nutrient powerhouse, is loaded with vitamins and minerals. This combo is designed to kickstart your weight management regime.*

Balance Booster: Papaya, Spinach, and Lemon Balm Burst

2 servings | 10 mins | 0 mins

Equipment

Blender, knife, cutting board.

Ingredients

- 1 medium papaya, peeled and seeded
- 2 cups of spinach
- A handful of lemon balm leaves

Nutritional information:
95 calories; 2g protein; 23g carbohydrates; 0.3g fat; 5g fiber; 0mg cholesterol; 30mg sodium; 430mg potassium.

Directions

1. Prepare the papaya by peeling and removing the seeds.
2. Wash the spinach and lemon balm leaves.
3. Combine all ingredients in a blender.
4. Blend until smooth and serve chilled.

Benefits*: Rich in digestive enzymes, papaya ensures a smooth digestion process. Spinach is packed with iron and other minerals, promoting blood health. The lemon balm has a calming effect, helping to reduce stress and anxiety and bringing a sense of balance to your body and mind.*

Slenderize Squeeze: Mango, Green Tea, and Basil Bliss

Equipment

Blender, knife, kettle

2 servings | 12 mins | 0 mins

Ingredients

- 1 ripe mango, peeled and pitted
- 1 cup brewed green tea, cooled
- A handful of fresh basil leaves

Nutritional information:
110 calories; 2g protein; 27g carbohydrates; 0.4g fat; 3g fiber; 0mg cholesterol; 5mg sodium; 340mg potassium.

Directions

1. Peel and pit the mango.
2. Allow the green tea to cool after brewing.
3. Combine mango, green tea, and basil leaves in a blender.
4. Blend until creamy, and enjoy immediately.

***Benefits**: Mangoes are a luscious source of vitamins, especially vitamin A. Green tea contains antioxidants and boosts metabolism, making it a key ingredient for weight loss. Basil offers anti-inflammatory benefits and a fresh, aromatic twist to this delightful blend.*

Torch & Tonic:

Apple, Red Cabbage, and Cayenne Combo

Equipment

2 servings | 10 mins | 0 mins

Blender, knife, cutting board

Directions

1. Core and slice the apples.
2. Roughly chop the red cabbage.
3. In a blender, combine apples, red cabbage, and cayenne pepper.
4. Blend until smooth and serve with a slice of apple on top.

Ingredients

- 2 medium apples, cored and sliced
- 1 cup red cabbage, chopped
- A pinch of cayenne pepper

Nutritional information:
105 calories; 1g protein; 28g carbohydrates; 0.2g fat; 6g fiber; 0mg cholesterol; 25mg sodium; 350mg potassium.

***Benefits**: Apples are high in dietary fiber, which aids with digestion. Red cabbage offers a wealth of antioxidants and vitamins. The cayenne pepper gives this juice a fiery kick while also helping to boost your metabolism and aid in fat burning.*

Immunity Boosters

Embark on a journey through the Immunity Boosters chapter, where each concoction serves as a shield for your health. Delve into recipes teeming with vital vitamins, minerals, and antioxidants known to fortify the body's defenses. Here, we blend the potent powers of ingredients like ginger, citrus fruits, and berries to craft juices that not only tantalize the taste buds but also equip the body to fend off ailments. Embrace these vibrant elixirs and empower your immune system to thrive.

Defense Dynamo: Kiwi, Spinach, and Ginger Groove

2 servings | 10 mins | 0 mins

Equipment

Juicer, sharp knife, chopping board

Ingredients

- 2 ripe kiwis
- 2 cups fresh spinach
- 1-inch piece of ginger, peeled

Nutritional information:
120 calories; 2g protein; 29g carbohydrates; 0.5g fat; 4g fiber; 0mg cholesterol; 20mg sodium; 400mg potassium.

Directions

1. Wash all the ingredients thoroughly.
2. Peel the kiwis and chop them into chunks.
3. Feed the kiwi chunks, spinach, and ginger into the juicer.
4. Pour out the juice into glasses and enjoy immediately.

***Benefits**: This delightful blend harmonizes the zesty zing of kiwi with the nutritious punch of spinach and the spicy undertones of ginger. It is a great choice to bolster the immune system, stimulate digestion, and offer a dose of vital vitamins..*

Protection Potion: Blueberry, Lemon, and Echinacea Essence

Equipment

Juicer, sharp knife, chopping board

3 servings | 12 mins | 0 mins

Directions

1. Wash the blueberries and lemon.
2. Chop the lemon into wedges.
3. Juice the blueberries and lemon wedges together.
4. Stir in the echinacea drops before serving.

Ingredients

- 2 cups blueberries
- 1 lemon, peeled
- 5 drops of echinacea tincture

Nutritional information:
140 calories; 1g protein; 35g carbohydrates; 0.7g fat; 5g fiber; 0mg cholesterol; 10mg sodium; 350mg potassium.

Benefits: *: Dive into a mix rich in antioxidants from blueberries, bolstered by vitamin C from lemon, and enhanced by the immune-supporting qualities of echinacea. This potion is tailor-made to offer protective benefits against colds and flu.*

Barrier Brew: Pomegranate, Beetroot, and Aloe Vera Affinity

2 servings | 15 mins | 0 mins

Equipment

Juicer, sharp knife, chopping board

Ingredients

- Seeds from 1 pomegranate
- 1 medium-sized beetroot, peeled
- 2 tablespoons aloe vera gel

Directions

1. Extract seeds from the pomegranate.
2. Chop the beetroot into small pieces.
3. Combine pomegranate seeds, beetroot, and aloe vera gel in the juicer.
4. Serve the vibrant red juice in chilled glasses.

Nutritional information:
160 calories; 3g protein; 37g carbohydrates; 0.6g fat; 6g fiber; 0mg cholesterol; 40mg sodium; 500mg potassium.

Benefits: *: A concoction designed to enhance skin health, promote better digestion, and strengthen the body's natural barriers. The mix combines the antioxidant prowess of pomegranate with the earthy taste of beetroot, complemented by the soothing properties of aloe vera.*

Shielding Splash: Strawberry, Basil, and Elderberry Euphoria

Equipment

Juicer, sharp knife, chopping board

Ingredients

- 2 cups strawberries
- A handful of fresh basil leaves
- 1 tablespoon elderberry syrup

Nutritional information:
130 calories; 2g protein; 31g carbohydrates; 0.8g fat; 5g fiber; 0mg cholesterol; 15mg sodium; 420mg potassium.

4 servings | 10 mins | 0 mins

Directions

1. Wash and hull the strawberries.
2. Gently rinse the basil leaves.
3. Juice the strawberries and basil together.
4. Stir in the elderberry syrup and pour into glasses.

Benefits: *: A summery delight that's not just for the warm months. Strawberries bring in a burst of vitamin C, basil offers anti-inflammatory properties, and elderberries are known for their immune-boosting characteristics*

Fortifying Fusion: Mango, Kale, and Black Pepper Punch

4 servings | 10 mins | 0 mins

Equipment

Juicer, sharp knife, chopping board, pepper mill

Ingredients

- 1 ripe mango, peeled and pitted
- 2 cups fresh kale leaves
- A pinch of freshly ground black pepper

Nutritional information:
160 calories; 3g protein; 38g carbohydrates; 1g fat; 5g fiber; 0mg cholesterol; 25mg sodium; 490mg potassium.

Directions

1. Wash the kale thoroughly.
2. Chop the mango into chunks suitable for juicing.
3. Feed the mango chunks and kale leaves into the juicer.
4. Pour into glasses, sprinkle with black pepper, and stir well before drinking.

***Benefits**: Dive into the tropical taste of mango paired with the nutrient-dense kale, finished with a kick of black pepper. This blend is a powerhouse for immune support, enhanced digestion, and is rich in vitamins A, C, and K.*

Resilience Refresher: Raspberry, Lemon Balm, and Chia Seed Symphony

Equipment

3 servings | 12 mins | 0 mins

Juicer, sharp knife, chopping board

Ingredients

- 2 cups raspberries
- A handful of fresh lemon balm leaves
- 2 tablespoons chia seeds

Nutritional information:
140 calories; 4g protein; 28g carbohydrates; 3g fat; 8g fiber; 0mg cholesterol; 5mg sodium; 350mg potassium.

Directions

1. Wash the raspberries and lemon balm leaves.
2. Juice the raspberries and lemon balm leaves together.
3. Pour into glasses, mix in the chia seeds, and let sit for 10 minutes before consuming.

***Benefits**: The tantalizing tartness of raspberries meets the calming notes of lemon balm in this refresher. Chia seeds add a dose of omega-3s, making this a holistic beverage for cognitive function, heart health, and immune defense.*

Vitality Verve: Green Apple, Spinach, and Rosehip Rally

Equipment

2 servings | 10 mins | 0 mins

Juicer, sharp knife, chopping board

Ingredients

- 2 green apples
- 2 cups fresh spinach
- 1 tablespoon rosehip powder or syrup

Nutritional information:
120 calories; 2g protein; 31g carbohydrates; 0.5g fat; 5g fiber; 0mg cholesterol; 20mg sodium; 420mg potassium.

Directions

1. Wash the apples and spinach.
2. Core and chop the apples into juicer-friendly pieces.
3. Juice the apples and spinach.
4. Pour into glasses and mix in the rosehip for an immunity-boosting treat.

Benefits: *Dive into an invigorating blend that rallies your defenses. The tartness of green apple complements iron-rich spinach, while rosehip packs a punch of vitamin C to keep immunity in top form.*

Strength Sip: Pineapple, Cilantro, and Goji Berry Gala

4 servings 15 mins 0 mins

Equipment

Juicer, sharp knife, chopping board

Ingredients

- 1/2 a pineapple, peeled and cored
- A handful of cilantro leaves
- 2 tablespoons goji berries

Nutritional information:
170 calories; 3g protein; 41g carbohydrates; 0.6g fat; 4g fiber; 0mg cholesterol; 10mg sodium; 480mg potassium.

Directions

1. Chop the pineapple into juicer-appropriate sizes.
2. Rinse the cilantro leaves thoroughly.
3. Juice the pineapple and cilantro together.
4. Pour into glasses, sprinkle with goji berries, and let sit for a few minutes before enjoying.

***Benefits**: Enjoy a sip of strength with the tropical allure of pineapple, the detoxifying properties of cilantro, and the superfood status of goji berries. This drink promises to elevate energy, support eye health, and reinforce immunity.*

Warrior Wave: Watermelon, Mint, and Eucalyptus Echo

2 servings | 10 mins | 0 mins

Equipment

Juicer, sharp knife, chopping board

Ingredients

- Half a medium-sized watermelon
- A handful of fresh mint leaves
- 1-2 drops of eucalyptus essential oil (food-grade)

Nutritional information:
90 calories; 2g protein; 22g carbohydrates; 0.3g fat; 1g fiber; 0mg cholesterol; 3mg sodium; 310mg potassium.

Directions

1. Slice the watermelon into chunks, discarding the rind.
2. Wash the mint leaves.
3. Juice the watermelon chunks and mint leaves.
4. Pour into glasses, add eucalyptus oil to each, stir, and enjoy.

***Benefits**: Unleash the warrior within with this hydrating blend. Watermelon provides ample hydration, mint soothes the digestive system, and a hint of eucalyptus promotes respiratory health, making this an all-around immunity champion.*

Immune Igniter: Grapefruit, Flaxseed, and Ginger Glow

2 servings | 10 mins | 0 mins

Equipment

Juicer, sharp knife, chopping board, grinder (for flaxseed)

Ingredients

- 2 grapefruits, peeled
- 1-inch piece of ginger, peeled
- 2 tablespoons ground flaxseeds

Nutritional information:
120 calories; 3g protein; 26g carbohydrates; 3g fat; 4g fiber; 0mg cholesterol; 10mg sodium; 370mg potassium.

Directions

1. Chop the grapefruits into chunks that fit into your juicer.
2. Feed the grapefruit chunks and ginger into the juicer.
3. Pour the juice into glasses, stir in the ground flaxseeds, and enjoy immediately.

***Benefits**: Jumpstart your immune response with the zesty combination of grapefruit and ginger. Flaxseeds add omega-3s, promoting heart health and aiding inflammation reduction.*

Health Hero: Cherry, Arugula, and Manuka Honey Harmony

Equipment

2 servings 12 mins 0 mins

Juicer, sharp knife, chopping board, grinder (for flaxseed)

Directions

1. Wash the cherries and arugula thoroughly.
2. Juice the cherries and arugula.
3. Pour the juice into glasses, stir in the Manuka honey, and savor the healthful benefits.

Ingredients

- 2 cups cherries, pitted
- 2 handfuls of arugula
- 2 teaspoons Manuka honey

Nutritional information:
140 calories; 2g protein; 34g carbohydrates; 0.5g fat; 3g fiber; 0mg cholesterol; 15mg sodium; 420mg potassium.

***Benefits**: Dive into the antioxidant-rich world of cherries combined with the peppery zest of arugula. A touch of Manuka honey sweetens the deal and brings in antimicrobial properties.*

Bulletproof Blend: Blackberry, Cucumber, and Thyme Thrill

Equipment

Juicer, sharp knife, chopping board

2 servings | 10 mins | 0 mins

Directions

1. Wash the blackberries, cucumber, and thyme.
2. Chop the cucumber into juicer-friendly pieces.
3. Feed the blackberries, cucumber chunks, and thyme into the juicer.
4. Pour the vibrant blend into glasses and enjoy the fortifying sip.

Ingredients

- 2 cups blackberries
- 1 medium cucumber
- A few sprigs of fresh thyme

Nutritional information:
110 calories; 3g protein; 25g carbohydrates; 1g fat; 5g fiber; 0mg cholesterol; 10mg sodium; 390mg potassium.

Benefits: *Arm yourself against pathogens with this refreshing blend. Blackberries offer antioxidants, cucumber hydrates, and thyme acts as an antimicrobial agent, ensuring a fortified immune system.*

Guarded Gulp: Lychee, Broccoli, and Cinnamon Concerto

Equipment

2 servings | 10 mins | 0 mins

Juicer, sharp knife, chopping board

Directions

1. Wash the lychee and broccoli thoroughly.
2. Chop the broccoli into juicer-compatible pieces.
3. Feed the lychee and broccoli chunks into the juicer.
4. Pour the juice into glasses, sprinkle in the cinnamon, stir, and drink up!

Ingredients

- 1 cup of lychee, pitted
- 1 medium-sized broccoli head
- A pinch of ground cinnamon

Nutritional information:
130 calories; 4g protein; 31g carbohydrates; 0.7g fat; 4g fiber; 0mg cholesterol; 30mg sodium; 460mg potassium.

Benefits: *The sweetness of lychee merges harmoniously with nutrient-dense broccoli, while a hint of cinnamon adds warmth and antiviral properties. This drink ensures a protective barrier against common illnesses*

Steadfast Smoothie: Passionfruit, Dandelion, and Lemon Liaison

2 servings 12 mins 0 mins

Equipment

Juicer, sharp knife, chopping board

Ingredients

- 3 passionfruits, halved and scooped
- 1 cup dandelion greens, washed
- Juice of 1 lemon

Nutritional information:
90 calories; 2g protein; 22g carbohydrates; 0.5g fat; 3g fiber; 0mg cholesterol; 20mg sodium; 400mg potassium.

Directions

1. Halve the passionfruits and scoop out the pulp.
2. Combine the passionfruit pulp, dandelion greens, and lemon juice in a blender.
3. Blend until smooth, pour into glasses, and savor the steadfast immunity boost.

***Benefits**: Passionfruit's tropical tang finds its match in the bitter greens of dandelion, offering a detoxifying effect. Lemon adds vitamin C and zest, making this blend a stalwart defender of your health.*

Energy Enhancers

Step into the invigorating realm of Energy Enhancers, where every blend is a burst of vitality in a glass. This chapter unravels a selection of juices designed to uplift your spirits, recharge your stamina, and propel you through the day. These concoctions are designed to deliver prolonged vigor without the jitters associated with caffeine by utilizing the natural energy sources of components such as green vegetables, tropical fruits, and nuts. Dive in and discover the delicious path to boundless energy and enthusiasm.

Dynamic Drive: Green Apple, Spinach, and Ginger Gust

2 servings | 7 mins | 0 mins

Equipment

Juicer, sharp knife, strainer

Ingredients

- 2 green apples, cored and sliced
- 2 cups of fresh spinach, washed
- 1 inch of ginger root, peeled

Nutritional information:
111 calories; 1.5g protein; 27g carbohydrates; 0.5g fat; 4g fiber; 0mg cholesterol; 20mg sodium; 255mg potassium.

Directions

1. Prep the ingredients by washing, coring, and slicing.
2. Start by juicing the green apples.
3. Add the spinach to the juicer.
4. Finish with the ginger root.
5. Pour into glasses, stir, and enjoy immediately.

***Benefits**: The Dynamic Drive is your daily dose of vitality. Green apples offer a fresh tartness packed with dietary fiber and vitamins. Spinach infuses the drink with iron, boosting hemoglobin levels. Ginger introduces a zesty spark, promoting digestion and combating inflammation.*

Energize Elixir: Blackberry, Orange, and Mint Mingle

Equipment

Juicer, sharp knife, strainer

3 servings | 8 mins | 0 mins

Ingredients

- 1 cup of blackberries
- 2 large oranges, peeled
- 10 mint leaves

Nutritional information:
95 calories; 2g protein; 22g carbohydrates; 0.3g fat; 3.5g fiber; 0mg cholesterol; 5mg sodium; 215mg potassium.

Directions

1. Begin by juicing the blackberries and oranges.
2. Mint leaves should be muddled at the bottom of the serving cups.
3. Pour the juice over the muddled mint.
4. Stir and enjoy for a refreshing boost.

***Benefits**: The Energize Elixir is an intoxicating blend to jump-start your mornings. Blackberries bring antioxidants, fostering cellular protection. Oranges, rich in vitamin C, bolster immune defenses. Mint freshens up the palate, aiding digestion and adding a cooling effect.*

Pep Power Potion: Watermelon, Basil, and Chia Seed Symphony

Equipment

4 servings | 10 mins | 0 mins

Blender, knife, mixing bowl

Ingredients

- 4 cups of watermelon cubes
- 8 basil leaves
- 2 tablespoons of chia seeds

Nutritional information:
90 calories; 2g protein; 18g carbohydrates; 1.5g fat; 4g fiber; 0mg cholesterol; 10mg sodium; 240mg potassium.

Directions

1. Blend the watermelon cubes and basil leaves in a blender.
2. Blend until smooth.
3. Pour out into a mixing bowl and add chia seeds, stirring well.
4. Allow it to sit for 10 minutes so the chia seeds can expand.
5. Serve in glasses with ice, if desired.

***Benefits**: The Pep Power Potion is a hydrating masterpiece. Watermelon, with its high water content, hydrates and offers essential vitamins. Basil infuses a herbal depth known for its adaptogenic properties. Chia seeds introduce fiber, protein, and omega-3s, making this a well-rounded energizer*

Zest Zenith: Blueberry, Acai, and Lime Lush

Equipment

2 servings 7 mins 0 mins

Juicer, sharp knife, strainer

Ingredients

- 1 cup of blueberries
- 2 packets (100g each) of acai puree
- Juice of 2 limes

Nutritional information:
120 calories; 1g protein; 28g carbohydrates; 0.5g fat; 3.5g fiber; 0mg cholesterol; 10mg sodium; 180mg potassium.

Directions

1. Start with juicing the blueberries.
2. Thaw and blend the acai puree until smooth.
3. Combine blueberry juice, acai, and lime juice.
4. Stir well, pour out into glasses, and serve immediately.

***Benefits**: The Zest Zenith is an antioxidant powerhouse. Blueberries combat oxidative stress, while acai provides a unique tropical richness and antioxidant benefits. Lime adds a tangy twist, loaded with Vitamin C, promoting glowing skin and boosting the immune system*

Stamina Surge: Pomegranate, Arugula, and Lemon Liaison

Equipment

Juicer, knife

3 servings | 9 mins | 0 mins

Directions

1. Begin with juicing the pomegranate seeds.
2. Add the arugula to the juicer.
3. Finish with the lemon juice, stirring well.
4. Pour into glasses and enjoy the vibrant surge.

Ingredients

- Seeds of 2 pomegranates
- 2 cups of arugula
- Juice of 1 lemon

Nutritional information:
110 calories; 2.5g protein; 26g carbohydrates; 0.3g fat; 3g fiber; 0mg cholesterol; 15mg sodium; 310mg potassium.

Benefits: *The Stamina Surge offers cardiovascular benefits while invigorating your senses. Pomegranates support heart health and are rich in antioxidants. With its peppery kick, Arugula is loaded with nitrates, enhancing athletic performance. Lemon brightens the blend, aiding digestion and adding zest.*

Boosted Brew: Kiwi, Cucumber, and Cayenne Clink

Equipment

2 servings 8 mins 0 mins

Blender, knife

Directions

1. Blend the peeled kiwis and cucumber until smooth.
2. Pour the mix into a jug and sprinkle in cayenne pepper.
3. Stir thoroughly, pour into glasses, and enjoy with a zing.

Ingredients

- 3 kiwis, peeled
- 1 large cucumber
- A pinch of cayenne pepper

Nutritional information:
90 calories; 2g protein; 20g carbohydrates; 0.5g fat; 4g fiber; 0mg cholesterol; 10mg sodium; 390mg potassium.

Benefits: *The Boosted Brew is a hydration hero with a fiery finish. Kiwi offers a sweet-tart flavor packed with Vitamin C and dietary fiber. Cucumber ensures skin hydration and replenishes essential minerals. Cayenne provides a spicy kick, stimulating metabolism and aiding in detoxification.*

Momentum Mix: Mango, Carrot, and Turmeric Tango

Equipment

Juicer, sharp knife, strainer

3 servings | 10 mins | 0 mins

Ingredients

- 2 ripe mangoes, peeled and pitted
- 4 large carrots
- ½ tsp of ground turmeric or 1-inch turmeric root

Nutritional information:
135 calories; 2g protein; 32g carbohydrates; 0.7g fat; 4g fiber; 0mg cholesterol; 70mg sodium; 390mg potassium.

Directions

1. Start by juicing the peeled mangoes.
2. Proceed to juice the carrots.
3. Add the ground turmeric or freshly juiced turmeric root.
4. Stir well, pour out into glasses, and serve immediately.

***Benefits**: Revel in a tropically sweet mix that also fortifies your health. Mangoes provide a summery sweetness and boost digestion and eye health. Carrots are a beta-carotene goldmine, promoting better vision and skin. Turmeric, with its curcumin content, acts as an anti-inflammatory and antioxidant agent, complementing the fruity duo.*

Lively Lift: Raspberry, Celery, and Goji Berry Bliss

Equipment

Juicer, knife

2 servings | 8 mins | 0 mins

Directions

1. Begin by juicing the raspberries and celery.
2. Add the softened goji berries to the juicer.
3. Stir the mixture well, pour into glasses, and savor the uplifting flavors.

Ingredients

- 1 cup of raspberries
- 3 celery stalks
- 2 tbsp of goji berries, soaked for 10 mins

Nutritional information:
120 calories; 3g protein; 28g carbohydrates; 0.5g fat; 5g fiber; 0mg cholesterol; 80mg sodium; 410mg potassium.

Benefits: *A berry-licious blend that invigorates and nourishes. Raspberries are antioxidant-rich, supporting heart health and providing anti-aging benefits. Celery offers hydration while balancing sodium levels. Goji berries, a superfood, enhance energy and mood and boost the immune system.*

Charge-Up Chug: Grapefruit, Broccoli, and Black Pepper Pulse

Equipment

Blender, knife

2 servings | 7 mins | 0 mins

Directions

1. Blend the grapefruit and broccoli until smooth.
2. Pour the mix into a jug and sprinkle in the black pepper.
3. Stir thoroughly, pour into glasses, and start your day with a charged-up spirit.

Ingredients

- 1 large grapefruit, peeled and seeded
- 1 cup of broccoli florets
- A pinch of freshly ground black pepper

Nutritional information:
100 calories; 3.5g protein; 24g carbohydrates; 0.4g fat; 6g fiber; 0mg cholesterol; 30mg sodium; 440mg potassium.

Benefits: *Experience a tangy and peppery concoction that ignites energy. Grapefruits, with their tangy zest, can aid in weight loss and insulin resistance. Broccoli, a cruciferous veggie, is a powerhouse of nutrients, offering Vitamin C, K, and much more. Black pepper enhances nutrient absorption, which is particularly beneficial for harnessing the full power of turmeric.*

Rise & Radiate: Strawberry, Maca, and Aloe Vera Rave

Equipment

2 servings | 10 mins | 0 mins

Blender, knife

Directions

1. Blend the strawberries until smooth.
2. Add the maca powder and aloe vera gel to the blender.
3. Blend again until all ingredients are well combined. Pour into glasses and serve fresh.

Ingredients

- 1 cup of fresh strawberries
- 1 tbsp of maca powder
- 2 tbsp of aloe vera gel

Nutritional information:
90 calories; 2g protein; 21g carbohydrates; 0.5g fat; 3g fiber; 0mg cholesterol; 5mg sodium; 220mg potassium.

***Benefits**: Dive into a blend that combines sweet flavors with holistic health benefits. Strawberries, packed with antioxidants, boost heart health and skin vibrancy. Maca, a famed energy enhancer, also balances hormones and boosts mood. Aloe vera soothes digestion and hydrates, making this a perfectly rounded morning elixir.*

Vigorous Vitality: Cherry, Fennel, and Matcha Marvel

Equipment

Blender, knife

3 servings | 10 mins | 0 mins

Directions

1. Blend the cherries and fennel until smooth.
2. Sprinkle in the matcha powder and blend again until evenly distributed. Pour, sip, and rejuvenate.

Ingredients

- 1 cup of cherries (pitted)
- ½ fennel bulb
- 1 tsp of matcha powder

Nutritional information:
110 calories; 2.5g protein; 25g carbohydrates; 1g fat; 4g fiber; 0mg cholesterol; 10mg sodium; 350mg potassium.

Benefits*: Relish in a unique combination that brings both energy and tranquility. Cherries are rich in antioxidants and promote better sleep. Fennel aids digestion, while matcha provides calm alertness due to L-theanine, making this an ideal midday pick-me-up.*

Sprint Spirit: Pineapple, Cilantro, and Coconut Concert

Equipment

2 servings | 10 mins | 0 mins

Blender, knife

Directions

1. Combine the pineapple chunks and cilantro in the blender.
2. Pour in the coconut water and blend until smooth. Serve chilled for a refreshing energy boost.

Ingredients

- 1 cup of pineapple chunks
- A sprig of fresh cilantro leaves
- ¼ cup of coconut water

Nutritional information:
95 calories; 1.5g protein; 23g carbohydrates; 0.4g fat; 2g fiber; 0mg cholesterol; 60mg sodium; 320mg potassium.

***Benefits**: This tropical melody is a rejuvenation in a glass. Pineapples, with their bromelain content, assist digestion and reduce inflammation. Cilantro detoxifies, while coconut hydrates and provides essential electrolytes. This blend promises to revive and replenish after physical exertion.*

Jolt Juice: Lemon, Wheatgrass, and Ginger Jive

2 servings | 8 mins | 0 mins

Equipment

Juicer, knife

Ingredients

- 1 large lemon, peeled
- 1 inch of ginger root
- 2 tbsp of wheatgrass

Nutritional information:
40 calories; 1g protein; 10g carbohydrates; 0.2g fat; 2g fiber; 0mg cholesterol; 5mg sodium; 130mg potassium.

Directions

1. Juice the lemon and ginger root together.
2. Mix in the wheatgrass until well combined. Serve immediately for a refreshing jolt of energy.

***Benefits**: Boost your metabolism and detoxify with this tangy and spicy blend. Lemons are packed with vitamin C and aid digestion, wheatgrass offers chlorophyll and a myriad of vitamins, while ginger, a renowned anti-inflammatory, adds a zing and promotes gut health.*

Recharge Refresher: Passionfruit, Spinach, and Flaxseed Flow

Equipment

Blender, knife

2 servings | 10 mins | 0 mins

Directions

1. Blend the passionfruit pulp and spinach until smooth.
2. Add in the flaxseed and blend again until everything is well mixed. Serve chilled, and feel recharged.

Ingredients

- 2 passionfruits, halved and scooped
- 1 cup of spinach
- 1 tbsp of ground flaxseed

Nutritional information:
90 calories; 3g protein; 19g carbohydrates; 2g fat; 5g fiber; 0mg cholesterol; 40mg sodium; 260mg potassium..

Benefits*: A delightful blend that's both tangy and earthy. Passionfruit enriches with antioxidants and dietary fiber, spinach brings iron and calcium into the mix, and flaxseed, a source of Omega-3 fatty acids, contributes to heart health and reduces inflammation.*

Burst & Bloom: Pear, Hibiscus, and Cinnamon Celebration

Equipment

Blender, knife

2 servings | 10 mins | 0 mins

Directions

1. Blend the pear until smooth.
2. Infuse the hibiscus petals in hot water for about 5 minutes, strain, and then add to the blender.
3. Add a pinch of cinnamon and blend everything. Serve with a sprinkle of cinnamon on top.

Ingredients

- 1 ripe pear, cored
- 1 tsp dried hibiscus petals
- A pinch of cinnamon

Nutritional information:
100 calories; 1g protein; 27g carbohydrates; 0.3g fat; 6g fiber; 0mg cholesterol; 5mg sodium; 215mg potassium.

Benefits*: Revel in a naturally sweet and subtly spiced drink. Pears are abundant in dietary fiber, promoting gut health. Hibiscus lowers blood pressure and boasts antioxidants. Meanwhile, cinnamon adds a dash of warmth and regulates blood sugar levels*

Digestive Aids

Navigate through the Digestive Aids Juice chapter, a haven for those seeking solace for their gut health. These crafted blends are rich in enzymes, fibers, and soothing herbs designed to promote optimal digestion, alleviate bloating, and provide gut-friendly nutrients. Drawing from ingredients like ginger, peppermint, and fiber-rich greens, this chapter offers beverages that satiate and harmonize your digestive system's intricate dance. Embark on a flavorful journey to digestive well-being with each rejuvenating sip.

Digestive Delight: Pineapple, Ginger, and Mint Mingle

Equipment

3 servings | 15 mins | 0 mins

Juicer, sharp knife, chopping board

Directions

1. Start by prepping your fruits: peel the pineapple and ginger.
2. Cut the pineapple into chunks that will fit your juicer.
3. Place mint leaves, pineapple chunks, and ginger into the juicer.
4. Juice until you've extracted as much liquid as possible.
5. Stir well and pour out into glasses to serve.

Ingredients

- 1 medium-sized pineapple, peeled and chopped
- 1-inch piece of ginger, peeled
- A handful of fresh mint leaves

Nutritional information:
120 calories; 1g protein; 30g carbohydrates; 0.5g fat; 2g fiber; 0mg cholesterol; 5mg sodium; 250mg potassium.

Benefits: *Revel in a concoction that's a true ally to your digestive system. Pineapples are high in bromelain, an enzyme that aids in protein digestion. Ginger, revered globally, not only adds zing but also boasts anti-inflammatory and gastrointestinal relief properties. Mint, refreshing and soothing, is known to ease indigestion and reduce symptoms like bloating. Together, this trio promises a delightfully smooth digestive journey*

Belly Bliss Brew: Papaya, Lemon, and Chamomile Combo

Equipment

Juicer, kettle, sharp knife, chopping board

2 servings | 12 mins | 0 mins

Directions

1. Begin by preparing the papaya: peel, deseed, and cut into suitable pieces.
2. Juice the papaya chunks.
3. Combine the lemon juice and papaya juice in a mixing bowl.
4. Allow the chamomile tea to cool after brewing. Mix it with the fruit juices.
5. Stir well, pour into glasses, and savor.

Ingredients

- 1 medium-sized papaya, peeled and deseeded
- Juice of 1 lemon
- 1 chamomile tea bag

Nutritional information:
90 calories; 1g protein; 22g carbohydrates; 0.3g fat; 3g fiber; 0mg cholesterol; 4mg sodium; 220mg potassium.

***Benefits**: Unwind with this blend designed for gut contentment. Papayas are equipped with papain, a digestive enzyme that helps break down proteins. The citrusy goodness of lemon aids in pH balance and detoxification. Chamomile, a tranquil herb, offers anti-inflammatory benefits, reducing stomach discomfort. This brew is a symphony of ingredients, ensuring a harmonious digestive process.*

Soothe & Smooth: Cucumber, Apple, and Basil Blend

Equipment

Juicer, sharp knife, chopping board

Ingredients

- 1 large cucumber
- 2 green apples
- A handful of fresh basil leaves

Nutritional information:
85 calories; 1g protein; 20g carbohydrates; 0.2g fat; 3g fiber; 0mg cholesterol; 8mg sodium; 180mg potassium.

3 servings | 10 mins | 0 mins

Directions

1. Wash and chop the cucumber and apples into sizes fit for the juicer.
2. Place basil leaves, cucumber pieces, and apple chunks into the juicer.
3. Extract the juice until all ingredients are processed.
4. Stir the blend, pour into glasses, and serve immediately.

Benefits: *Immerse in a refreshing potion primed to pacify your stomach. Cucumbers are naturally hydrating, making them perfect for promoting detoxification. Apples, packed with dietary fiber, ensure smooth bowel movements. Basil, with its anti-inflammatory and adaptogenic properties, soothes the digestive tract. Together, they provide a serene, smoothing experience for your belly.*

Tummy Tonic: Carrot, Peppermint, and Chia Seed Symphony

Equipment

Juicer, blender, sharp knife, chopping board

Ingredients

- 3 large carrots
- 10 fresh peppermint leaves
- 1 tablespoon chia seeds
- 1 cup of water

Nutritional information:
95 calories; 2g protein; 18g carbohydrates; 2.5g fat; 5g fiber; 0mg cholesterol; 60mg sodium; 300mg potassium.

2 servings | 15 mins | 0 mins

Directions

1. Clean and chop the carrots into sizes suitable for the juicer.
2. Juice the carrots.
3. In a blender, combine carrot juice, peppermint leaves, chia seeds, and water.
4. Blend until smooth.
5. Pour into glasses, allow it to sit for a couple of minutes for the chia seeds to expand slightly, and then enjoy.

***Benefits**: Dive into a drink that caters to the core of your digestive well-being. Carrots are dense in dietary fiber, promoting a healthy gut. Peppermint is widely acknowledged for alleviating IBS symptoms and general stomach upsets. Chia seeds, with their fiber-rich profile, ensure regular bowel movement. This concoction is a symphony that plays harmoniously for your tummy's tranquility.*

Gastric Grace: Mango, Turmeric, and Flaxseed Fusion

Equipment

Blender, knife, chopping board

Ingredients

- 1 ripe mango
- 1 teaspoon ground turmeric
- 1 tablespoon flaxseeds
- 1 cup of water

Nutritional information:
130 calories; 2g protein; 30g carbohydrates; 3g fat; 4g fiber; 0mg cholesterol; 10mg sodium; 250mg potassium.

2 servings · 15 mins · 0 mins

Directions

1. Peel, deseed and chop the mango into chunks.
2. In a blender, combine mango chunks, ground turmeric, flaxseeds, and water.
3. Blend until smooth and creamy.
4. Pour the mixture into glasses and enjoy immediately.

***Benefits**: Revel in the sweet richness of mango complemented by the anti-inflammatory wonders of turmeric. This fusion brings grace to your gastrointestinal tract. Mangoes, rich in digestive enzymes, facilitate effective digestion. Turmeric's curcumin content provides an anti-inflammatory boost, and flaxseeds, laden with fiber, further assist in smooth digestion.*

Relief Refresher: Watermelon, Cilantro, and Fennel Flow

3 servings | 12 mins | 0 mins

Equipment

Blender, knife, chopping board

Ingredients

- 2 cups of watermelon chunks
- A handful of cilantro leaves
- 1 teaspoon fennel seeds
- 1 cup of water (optional)

Nutritional information: 60 calories; 1g protein; 15g carbohydrates; 0.5g fat; 1g fiber; 0mg cholesterol; 5mg sodium; 210mg potassium.

Directions

1. Slice the watermelon and extract around 2 cups of chunks.
2. Clean the cilantro leaves thoroughly.
3. In a blender, combine watermelon chunks, cilantro, fennel seeds, and water if you prefer a lighter consistency.
4. Blend until smooth.
5. Pour the blend into glasses and savor immediately.

***Benefits**: Bask in the soothing essence of this refreshing blend designed to bring relief to the stomach. Watermelon hydrates and aids in flushing out toxins. Cilantro's natural detoxifying properties cleanse the system, while fennel aids in alleviating gas and bloating, ensuring a calm and relaxed digestive system.*

Gut Gem: Watermelon, Cilantro, and Fennel Flow

Equipment

Blender, knife, bowl

3 servings | 15 mins | 0 mins

Directions

1. Extract seeds from the pomegranate.
2. In a blender, combine pomegranate seeds, yogurt, and acai powder.
3. Blend until smooth and creamy.
4. Pour out the mixture into glasses and serve chilled.

Ingredients

- Seeds from 1 pomegranate
- 1 cup of yogurt (preferably probiotic-rich)
- 2 tablespoons acai powder

Nutritional information:
170 calories; 5g protein; 27g carbohydrates; 5g fat; 4g fiber; 10mg cholesterol; 40mg sodium; 300mg potassium.

Benefits: *Dive deep into this gut-enhancing gem that merges the antioxidant prowess of pomegranate with the gut flora benefits of yogurt. Acai adds an extra layer of antioxidant power, fortifying this blend as a must-have for a happy belly. This blend aids in smoother digestion, offers a rich dose of antioxidants, and promotes a healthier gut microbiome.*

Digestive Dance: Watermelon, Cilantro, and Fennel Flow

Equipment

3 servings | 10 mins | 0 mins

Blender, knife, chopping board

Directions

1. Peel and slice the kiwis.
2. Clean the spinach leaves thoroughly.
3. Chop the ginger root into small pieces.
4. In a blender, combine sliced kiwis, spinach, ginger, and water.
5. Blend until you achieve a smooth consistency.
6. Pour the blend into glasses and savor its refreshing taste.

Ingredients

- 2 ripe kiwis
- 1 cup of spinach leaves
- 1-inch ginger root
- 1 cup of water

Nutritional information:
70 calories; 2g protein; 17g carbohydrates; 0.5g fat; 3g fiber; 0mg cholesterol; 20mg sodium; 320mg potassium..

Benefits: *Glide into the dance of digestion with the mesmerizing blend of kiwi, spinach, and ginger. Kiwi, brimming with digestive enzymes, works wonders in breaking down food molecules. Spinach offers essential fiber to ensure smoother bowel movements and ginger's anti-inflammatory properties soothe the stomach, ensuring a harmonious digestive routine.*

Tranquil Tummy Twist:

Strawberry, Dandelion, and Aloe Essence

Equipment

2 servings | 10 mins | 0 mins

Blender, knife, bowl

Ingredients

- 1 cup of fresh strawberries
- 1/2 cup dandelion greens
- 2 tablespoons aloe vera gel

Nutritional information:
90 calories; 2g protein; 21g carbohydrates; 0.5g fat; 3g fiber; 0mg cholesterol; 10mg sodium; 340mg potassium.

Directions

1. Wash and hull the strawberries.
2. Cleanse the dandelion greens thoroughly.
3. In a blender, combine strawberries, dandelion greens, and aloe vera gel.
4. Blend until smooth.
5. Pour out the juice into glasses and enjoy immediately.

***Benefits**: This soothing blend provides a gentle relief to upset stomachs. Strawberries, rich in fiber and antioxidants, collaborate with dandelion's natural diuretic properties. Aloe essence, known for its digestive support, ensures a calm and tranquil tummy experience. It is an excellent choice after meals or for those with sensitive digestion.*

Bowel Balance: Strawberry, Dandelion, and Aloe Essence

Equipment

Blender, knife, chopping board

2 servings | 12 mins | 0 mins

Directions

1. Wash the blueberries thoroughly.
2. Chop the cabbage into small pieces.
3. In a blender, combine blueberries, chopped cabbage, and kefir.
4. Blend until you achieve a smooth consistency.
5. Pour the blend into glasses and savor its unique taste.

Ingredients

- 1 cup of fresh blueberries
- 1/2 cup chopped cabbage
- 1 cup of kefir (plain)

Nutritional information:
120 calories; 4g protein; 25g carbohydrates; 1g fat; 4g fiber; 5mg cholesterol; 50mg sodium; 360mg potassium.

***Benefits**: Achieve optimal bowel balance with this potent mix. Blueberries offer a bounty of antioxidants and fiber, aiding in smoother bowel movements. Cabbage, recognized for its gut-healing properties, pairs splendidly with kefir, a fermented drink teeming with probiotics. This blend promotes gut health, reduces bloating, and ensures regular bowel movements.*

Ease Elixir: Grape, Celery, and Lavender Lush

Equipment

Juicer, knife, strainer

2 servings | 10 mins | 0 mins

Directions

1. Thoroughly wash grapes and celery stalks.
2. Pass the grapes and celery through a juicer.
3. In a separate bowl, steep dried lavender in hot water for 5 minutes and then strain.
4. Mix the lavender infusion with the grape-celery juice.
5. Serve chilled, and relish the soothing experience.

Ingredients

- 1 cup of red grapes
- 2 celery stalks
- 1 teaspoon dried lavender buds

Nutritional information:
85 calories; 1g protein; 20g carbohydrates; 0.3g fat; 2g fiber; 0mg cholesterol; 45mg sodium; 320mg potassium.

Benefits: *A harmonious blend crafted for optimal digestive ease. The grapes provide natural sugars and essential vitamins, while the celery offers dietary fiber to promote smooth digestion. Lavender, a renowned soothing agent, helps reduce stomach discomfort and imparts a calming aroma, making every sip a delightful digestive respite.*

Stomach Soothe: Blackberry, Chamomile, and Green Tea Gala

Equipment

2 servings | 12 mins | 0 mins

Blender, teapot, strainer

Directions

1. Wash the blackberries meticulously.
2. Brew chamomile and green tea together in hot water for 5 minutes.
3. In a blender, combine the blackberries and the tea infusion.
4. Blend until a silky consistency is achieved.
5. Strain the blend to remove any blackberry seeds, then serve immediately.

Ingredients

- 1 cup of fresh blackberries
- 1 chamomile tea bag
- 1 green tea bag

Nutritional information:
60 calories; 1.5g protein; 15g carbohydrates; 0.2g fat; 3g fiber; 0mg cholesterol; 10mg sodium; 270mg potassium.

***Benefits**: Designed to nurture and comfort the stomach, this elixir is a blend of powerful ingredients. Blackberries, rich in fiber, assist in promoting digestive health. Chamomile and green tea, both known for their soothing properties, help in alleviating indigestion and inflammation, making this the perfect drink after a hearty meal.*

Skin and Beauty Blends

Immerse yourself in the Skin and Beauty Blends chapter, where radiance and well-being flow from within. Unveil a collection of juices teeming with antioxidants, hydrating elements, and essential vitamins tailored to rejuvenate skin, strengthen hair, and boost overall beauty. By incorporating ingredients like berries, cucumbers, and rosemary, these blends are more than just a feast for the taste buds; they're a beauty ritual in a glass. Let every sip be a step towards glowing skin and vibrant health

Radiance Reviver: Strawberry, Aloe Vera, and Lime Liaison

2 servings | 10 mins | 0 mins

Equipment

Blender

Ingredients

- 1 cup strawberries, hulled
- 2 tablespoons aloe vera gel
- Juice of 1 lime

Nutritional information:
85 calories; 2g protein; 20g carbohydrates; 0.5g fat; 3g fiber; 0mg cholesterol; 10mg sodium; 250mg potassium.

Directions

1. Place strawberries, aloe vera gel, and lime juice into the blender.
2. Blend until you achieve a smooth consistency.
3. Pour out into glasses and serve immediately for the best taste and maximum benefits.

***Benefits**: An exuberant blend bursting with antioxidants from strawberries, this concoction also harnesses the skin-soothing properties of aloe vera. The dash of lime not only adds a zesty flavor but also works to brighten the complexion and even out skin tone.*

Glowing Grace: Kiwi, Cucumber, and Rose Water Rhapsody

3 servings | 10 mins | 0 mins

Equipment

Juicer, Mixing bowl

Ingredients

- 3 ripe kiwis, peeled
- 1 medium cucumber
- 2 tablespoons rose water

Nutritional information:
80 calories; 2g protein; 18g carbohydrates; 0.3g fat; 4g fiber; 0mg cholesterol; 8mg sodium; 300mg potassium.

Directions

1. Juice the kiwis and cucumber using a juicer.
2. Pour out the juice into a mixing bowl and stir in the rose water.
3. Serve in glasses and enjoy the calming, beauty-boosting effects.

Benefits: *This refreshing blend combines the Vitamin C powerhouse, kiwi, with the hydrating properties of cucumber. Rose water adds a gentle, aromatic touch while aiding in reducing skin redness and inflammation.*

Silky Skin Sip: Kiwi, Cucumber, and Rose Water Rhapsody

2 servings | 8 mins | 0 mins

Equipment

Blender

Ingredients

- 2 ripe peaches, pitted and sliced
- ½ avocado, pitted and scooped
- 1 cup almond milk

Nutritional information:
170 calories; 4g protein; 20g carbohydrates; 10g fat; 6g fiber; 0mg cholesterol; 45mg sodium; 410mg potassium.

Directions

1. Combine peaches, avocado, and almond milk in the blender.
2. Blend till creamy and smooth.
3. Pour into glasses and savor the nourishing drink.

***Benefits**: This luxurious blend is a treat for the skin. Peaches provide hydration, avocados supply the skin with essential fatty acids, and almond milk offers additional moisturizing benefits. Together, they work to give the skin a soft, supple appearance.*

Lustrous Lush: Mango, Beetroot, and Hibiscus Harmony

Equipment

Blender

2 servings | 12 mins | 0 mins

Directions

1. Place the mango, beetroot, and hibiscus petals into the blender.
2. Blend until smooth and creamy.
3. Pour into glasses and serve chilled.

Ingredients

- 1 ripe mango, peeled and pitted
- 1 small beetroot, peeled and chopped
- 2 tablespoons dried hibiscus petals

Nutritional information:
120 calories; 3g protein; 28g carbohydrates; 0.5g fat; 5g fiber; 0mg cholesterol; 50mg sodium; 420mg potassium.

Benefits: *Dive into the tropical sweetness of mango coupled with the earthiness of beetroot. This mixture enhances your skin in addition to tantalizing your taste senses. The inclusion of hibiscus provides a natural source of AHAs, promoting a fresher, younger, and smoother-looking complexion.*

Dewy Dream: Watermelon, Celery, and Chia Seed Delight

Equipment

2 servings | 12 mins | 0 mins

Blender

Directions

1. Blend watermelon and celery until smooth.
2. Stir in chia seeds.
3. Let it sit for 10 minutes to allow the chia seeds to swell.
4. Serve and relish the dewy freshness.

Ingredients

- 2 cups watermelon cubes
- 2 celery stalks, chopped
- 2 tablespoons chia seeds

Nutritional information:
90 calories; 2g protein; 20g carbohydrates; 2g fat; 4g fiber; 0mg cholesterol; 45mg sodium; 320mg potassium.

Benefits: *The hydrating prowess of watermelon meets the mineral-rich celery in this rejuvenating drink. Omega-3 fatty acids, which are included in chia seeds, are believed to enhance skin health by lowering inflammation and dryness.*

Hydration Haven: Cactus Pear, Cilantro, and Coconut Water Concoction

Equipment

2 servings | 15 mins | 0 mins

Blender

Ingredients

- 2 cactus pears, peeled and seeds removed
- A handful of cilantro leaves
- 1 cup coconut water

Nutritional information:
100 calories; 2g protein; 23g carbohydrates; 1g fat; 5g fiber; 0mg cholesterol; 110mg sodium; 390mg potassium.

Directions

1. In the blender, combine cactus pear, cilantro, and coconut water.
2. Blend until smooth.
3. Strain if desired and serve cold.

***Benefits**: A unique blend that screams hydration at its best. Cactus pear, rich in skin-loving antioxidants, when combined with the detoxifying properties of cilantro and the hydration of coconut water, makes for a potent beauty beverage.*

Complexion Cure: Raspberry, Kale, and Collagen Collusion

Equipment

2 servings | 10 mins | 0 mins

Blender

Directions

1. Add raspberries, kale, and collagen powder to the blender.
2. Blend until smooth and thoroughly mixed.
3. Pour into glasses and consume immediately for best results.

Ingredients

- 1 cup raspberries
- 2 cups kale leaves, stems removed
- 2 scoops collagen powder

Nutritional information:
115 calories; 12g protein; 18g carbohydrates; 0.7g fat; 5g fiber; 0mg cholesterol; 45mg sodium; 370mg potassium.

***Benefits**: This blend is a triple threat to radiant skin. Raspberries provide vital vitamins and antioxidants, kale brings along a wave of detoxifying chlorophyll, and collagen is the key to youthful elasticity. Together, they promise a complexion that's vibrant and refreshed.*

Beauty Bliss: Apple, Rosehip, and Flaxseed Fusion

Equipment

Blender

2 servings | 12 mins | 0 mins

Ingredients

- 2 medium-sized apples, cored and chopped
- 1 tablespoon rosehip powder or 2 tablespoons dried rosehips
- 2 tablespoons flaxseeds, ground

Nutritional information:
135 calories; 3g protein; 28g carbohydrates; 3g fat; 6g fiber; 0mg cholesterol; 10mg sodium; 410mg potassium.

Directions

1. In the blender, combine apples, rosehip, and flaxseeds.
2. Blend until you achieve a smooth consistency.
3. Serve immediately and enjoy the rosy glow!

Benefits*: This drink is a beacon of skin health. Apples bring in a dose of vital nutrients, rosehip is rich in vitamin C for that collagen boost, and flaxseeds offer the goodness of omega-3s for skin hydration and glow.*

Eternal Elegance: Cherry, Pomegranate, and Goji Berry Gala

Equipment

2 servings | 15 mins | 0 mins

Blender

Ingredients

- 1 cup cherries, pitted
- 1 cup pomegranate seeds
- 2 tablespoons dried goji berries, soaked for 10 minutes

Directions

1. Combine cherries, pomegranate seeds, and soaked goji berries in the blender.
2. Blend until smooth and velvety.
3. Pour, serve, and bask in the skin-enhancing benefits.

Nutritional information:
120 calories; 2g protein; 27g carbohydrates; 0.5g fat; 4g fiber; 0mg cholesterol; 5mg sodium; 400mg potassium.

Benefits: *A delightful concoction of antioxidant-rich ingredients, this blend is the secret to eternal skin youthfulness. While cherries and pomegranates work on skin renewal, goji berries bring in the element of skin protection and rejuvenation.*

Youthful Yield: Acai, Banana, and Green Tea Grace

Equipment

2 servings | 10 mins | 5 mins

Blender, Teapot or kettle

Ingredients

- 1 acai berry packet or 1 cup frozen acai berries
- 1 ripe banana
- 1 cup brewed and cooled green tea

Nutritional information:
140 calories; 3g protein; 32g carbohydrates; 1g fat; 4g fiber; 0mg cholesterol; 7mg sodium; 480mg potassium..

Directions

1. Green tea should be brewed and allowed to cool.
2. In a blender, add the acai berries, banana, and cooled green tea.
3. Blend until smooth.
4. Pour into glasses and enjoy the youthful infusion.

***Benefits**: Harness the power of acai, a potent source of antioxidants, combined with banana's vitamins and green tea's catechins to battle free radicals, maintain skin elasticity, and prevent premature aging.*

Glow Getter: Passionfruit, Turmeric, and Lemon Lush

Equipment

2 servings | 10 mins | 0 mins

Blender, Teapot or kettle

Ingredients

- 2 passionfruits, halved and scooped
- 1 teaspoon turmeric powder
- Juice of 1 lemon

Nutritional information:
85 calories; 2g protein; 20g carbohydrates; 0.5g fat; 6g fiber; 0mg cholesterol; 10mg sodium; 310mg potassium.

Directions

1. Place passionfruit pulp, turmeric powder, and lemon juice in a blender.
2. Blend until everything is well combined.
3. Pour into glasses, and feel the immediate refreshment and skin benefits.

***Benefits**: This blend will light up your complexion from the inside out. Passionfruit's vitamin C, turmeric's anti-inflammatory properties, and lemon's detoxifying effects work harmoniously to give you that desired radiant glow.*

Skin Soiree: Pineapple, Spirulina, and Mint Mix

2 servings | 10 mins | 0 mins

Equipment

Blender

Ingredients

- 1 cup pineapple chunks
- 1 teaspoon spirulina powder
- A handful of fresh mint leaves

Nutritional information:
110 calories; 2g protein; 26g carbohydrates; 0.3g fat; 3g fiber; 0mg cholesterol; 15mg sodium; 290mg potassium.

Directions

1. In the blender, add pineapple chunks, spirulina powder, and mint leaves.
2. Blend until you get a smooth and velvety texture.
3. Serve chilled, and experience a burst of freshness with each sip.

***Benefits**: An exotic blend designed for skin vitality. Pineapple's enzymes promote clarity and brightness, spirulina provides deep nourishment with its proteins and vitamins, and mint revitalizes with its refreshing properties.*

Mind and Mood Modulators

Delve into the Mind and Mood Modulators chapter, a sanctuary for mental well-being and emotional equilibrium. Explore concoctions crafted to elevate mood, sharpen focus, and relieve stress, using nature's finest ingredients. With the potent synergy of adaptogens, brain-boosting berries, and calming herbs, these blends promise more than mere refreshment. They're a sensory journey towards a clearer mind and brighter spirits, offering serenity with every flavorful sip

Clarity Cocktail: Blueberry, Spinach, and Lavender Liaison

Equipment

2 servings | 10 mins | 0 mins

Blender

Directions

1. Rinse the blueberries and spinach thoroughly.
2. Add the blueberries, spinach, and dried lavender buds to the blender.
3. Blend until smooth.
4. Pour into glasses and enjoy.

Ingredients

- 1 cup of blueberries
- 2 cups of fresh spinach
- 1 teaspoon dried lavender buds

Nutritional information:
105 calories; 3g protein; 25g carbohydrates; 0.7g fat; 4g fiber; 0mg cholesterol; 40mg sodium; 320mg potassium..

Benefits: *Dive into the blend of blueberry and spinach, enriched with the calming aroma of lavender. This cocktail promotes mental clarity, offers antioxidant-rich nourishment, and calms the mind for optimal focus and alertness.*

Serenity Squeeze: Mango, Chamomile, and Almond Milk Symphony

Equipment

Blender

2 servings | 10 mins | 0 mins

Ingredients

- 1 ripe mango, peeled and pitted
- 1 chamomile tea bag
- 2 cups of almond milk

Nutritional information:
175 calories; 2g protein; 40g carbohydrates; 3g fat; 3g fiber; 0mg cholesterol; 150mg sodium; 450mg potassium.

Directions

1. Allow the chamomile tea to cool after brewing.
2. Add the mango chunks, cooled chamomile tea, and almond milk to the blender.
3. Blend until creamy and smooth.
4. Serve and drift into serenity.

***Benefits**: Relish the creamy embrace of mango and almond milk paired with the soothing notes of chamomile. This blend offers relaxation, alleviates stress, and helps in restoring tranquility and balance.*

Mood Marvel: Pomegranate, Oat Milk, and Rosemary Rhapsody

Equipment

Blender

2 servings | 10 mins | 0 mins

Directions

1. Remove the seeds from the pomegranate.
2. Add the pomegranate seeds, oat milk, and fresh rosemary to the blender.
3. Blend until everything is well combined.
4. Serve in glasses and savor the mood-enhancing marvel.

Ingredients

- Seeds of 1 pomegranate
- 2 cups of oat milk
- 1 sprig of fresh rosemary

Nutritional information:
190 calories; 5g protein; 42g carbohydrates; 3.5g fat; 6g fiber; 0mg cholesterol; 90mg sodium; 510mg potassium.

***Benefits**: Experience the delightful infusion of pomegranate seeds, satiating oat milk, and the aromatic touch of rosemary. This elixir aids cognitive functions, uplifts mood, and brings about a sense of rejuvenation and joy.*

Mindful Medley: Kiwi, Walnut, and Lemon Balm Blend

Equipment

Blender

2 servings | 10 mins | 0 mins

Directions

1. Prep the kiwis by peeling and slicing them.
2. Add kiwi slices, soaked walnuts, and lemon balm to the blender.
3. Blend until smooth.
4. Pour into glasses and relish the mindfulness it brings.

Ingredients

- 2 ripe kiwis, peeled and sliced
- 10 walnuts, soaked
- A few leaves of fresh lemon balm

Nutritional information:
210 calories; 4g protein; 27g carbohydrates; 11g fat; 5g fiber; 0mg cholesterol; 7mg sodium; 500mg potassium.

Benefits*: This refreshing blend of kiwi, crunchy walnut, and calming lemon balm is a sensory delight. Boosted with Vitamin C from kiwi, brain-health-promoting omega-3s from walnuts, and the soothing properties of lemon balm, it promotes mindfulness and focus.*

Tranquil Tonic: Cherry, Aloe Vera, and Vanilla Verve

Equipment

2 servings | 10 mins | 0 mins

Blender

Directions

1. Ensure cherries are pitted.
2. Add cherries, aloe vera gel, and vanilla extract to the blender.
3. Blend until velvety smooth.
4. Serve chilled for a tranquil experience.

Ingredients

- 1 cup of cherries (pitted)
- 2 tablespoons of pure aloe vera gel
- 1/2 teaspoon vanilla extract

Nutritional information:
115 calories; 1g protein; 28g carbohydrates; 0.5g fat; 2g fiber; 0mg cholesterol; 5mg sodium; 310mg potassium.

Benefits*: Dive into serenity with the sweet-tartness of cherries, skin-loving aloe vera, and aromatic vanilla. This tonic supports relaxation, soothes the digestive system, and tantalizes the tastebuds.*

Focus Fusion: Green Apple, Kale, and Matcha Mix

Equipment

Blender

Ingredients

- 2 green apples, cored and sliced
- 2 cups of fresh kale, destemmed
- 1 teaspoon matcha powder

Nutritional information:
130 calories; 2g protein; 32g carbohydrates; 1g fat; 5g fiber; 0mg cholesterol; 20mg sodium; 450mg potassium.

2 servings 10 mins 0 mins

Directions

1. Core and slice the apples.
2. Add apple slices, fresh kale, and matcha powder to the blender.
3. Blend until smooth and frothy.
4. Pour into glasses, and let the focus set in.

***Benefits**: This vibrant blend fuses the crispness of green apple, the nutrient richness of kale, and the caffeine kick of matcha. It's designed to sharpen focus, provide sustained energy, and supply essential vitamins and minerals.*

Elevate Elixir: Passionfruit, Flaxseed, and Ginger Groove

Equipment

Blender

2 servings | 8 mins | 0 mins

Directions

1. Scoop out the pulp from the passionfruits.
2. Add passionfruit pulp, ground flaxseed, and ginger to the blender.
3. Blend until well combined.
4. Pour into glasses and enjoy the elevated mood.

Ingredients

- 3 ripe passionfruits, halved and pulp extracted
- 2 tablespoons of ground flaxseed
- 1-inch piece of fresh ginger, peeled

Nutritional information:
185 calories; 3g protein; 35g carbohydrates; 5g fat; 8g fiber; 0mg cholesterol; 10mg sodium; 380mg potassium.

Benefits: *Passionfruit's tantalizing tartness dances with ginger's zest and flaxseed's nuttiness in this elixir. The vitamin-rich passionfruit boosts mood, flaxseeds offer omega-3s for brain health, and ginger aids digestion and circulation.*

Calm & Collected: Pineapple, Banana, and Ashwagandha Concerto

Equipment

2 servings | 10 mins | 0 mins

Blender

Directions

1. Place pineapple chunks, peeled bananas, and Ashwagandha powder in the blender.
2. Blend until smooth and creamy.
3. Pour into glasses and take a moment to savor the calmness.

Ingredients

- 1 cup of pineapple chunks
- 2 ripe bananas, peeled
- 1/2 teaspoon Ashwagandha powder

Nutritional information:
220 calories; 2g protein; 58g carbohydrates; 0.5g fat; 5g fiber; 0mg cholesterol; 5mg sodium; 590mg potassium.

Benefits: *Experience a state of calm with this soothing blend. Pineapple provides mood-lifting bromelain, bananas offer mood-stabilizing magnesium and potassium, while Ashwagandha, an adaptogen, helps combat stress.*

Joyful Jolt: Orange, Turmeric, and Mint Magic

2 servings | 8 mins | 0 mins

Equipment

Blender

Ingredients

- 2 large oranges, peeled and segmented
- 1/2 teaspoon ground turmeric
- 10 fresh mint leaves

Nutritional information:
130 calories; 2g protein; 32g carbohydrates; 0.5g fat; 4g fiber; 0mg cholesterol; 2mg sodium; 450mg potassium.

Directions

1. Add peeled orange segments, ground turmeric, and fresh mint leaves to the blender.
2. Blend until silky smooth.
3. Pour into glasses, take a sip, and embrace the joyful jolt.

***Benefits**: This citrusy concoction is a burst of sunshine in a glass. Oranges, packed with vitamin C, enhance mood and immunity. Turmeric's curcumin has anti-inflammatory properties, and mint adds a refreshing twist and aids digestion.*

Mind Muse: Raspberry, Cacao, and Maca Medley

Equipment

2 servings 8 mins 0 mins

Blender

Directions

1. Combine raspberries, cacao powder, and maca powder in the blender.
2. Add almond milk for creaminess.
3. Blend until smooth, ensuring the powders are well incorporated.
4. Pour into glasses and savor the muse.

Ingredients

- 1 cup of fresh raspberries
- 2 tablespoons cacao powder
- 1 teaspoon maca powder
- 1 cup of almond milk

Nutritional information:
170 calories; 4g protein; 27g carbohydrates; 7g fat; 9g fiber; 0mg cholesterol; 105mg sodium; 320mg potassium.

Benefits: *A marriage of delightful flavors and superfoods, this blend combines the antioxidants of raspberries with the mood-enhancing properties of cacao. Maca, often touted for its adaptogenic qualities, may help balance mood and boost energy.*

Zen Zest: Lemon, Chia, and Chamomile Charm

Equipment

2 servings | 10 mins | 0 mins

Blender

Directions

1. Combine lemon juice, chia seeds, and the contents of the chamomile tea bag in the blender.
2. Add cold water.
3. Blend until smooth and well-mixed.
4. Pour into glasses and enjoy a sip of serenity.

Ingredients

- Juice of 2 large lemons
- 2 tablespoons chia seeds
- 1 chamomile tea bag (contents emptied)
- 1 cup of cold water

Nutritional information:
90 calories; 3g protein; 14g carbohydrates; 4g fat; 8g fiber; 0mg cholesterol; 10mg sodium; 120mg potassium.

Benefits: *This soothing blend is designed to promote relaxation and reduce stress. Lemon provides a bright burst of flavor and vitamin C, chia seeds offer a boost of fiber and Omega-3s, and chamomile is renowned for its calming properties.*

Brain Boost Brew: Beetroot, Coconut Water, and Cinnamon Combo

Equipment

2 servings · 10 mins · 0 mins

Blender

Directions

1. Place chopped beetroot in the blender.
2. Add coconut water and ground cinnamon.
3. Blend until the mixture is smooth and the beetroot is fully pureed.
4. Pour into glasses and relish the refreshing brew.

Ingredients

- 1 medium beetroot, peeled and chopped
- 1 cup of coconut water
- 1/2 teaspoon ground cinnamon

Nutritional information:
80 calories; 2g protein; 18g carbohydrates; 0.5g fat; 4g fiber; 0mg cholesterol; 250mg sodium; 580mg potassium.

***Benefits**: This elixir is formulated to enhance cognitive function and hydration. Beetroots are rich in nitrates, improving blood flow to the brain. Coconut water provides hydration and electrolytes, while cinnamon can help regulate blood sugar.*

Heart Health Helpers

Welcome to the Heart Health Helpers chapter, a curated collection of blends dedicated to the rhythm of life. Here, you'll encounter recipes rich in antioxidants, fibers, and heart-loving nutrients, all aimed at bolstering cardiovascular resilience. Whether it's through the omega-rich flaxseeds or the potassium-packed bananas, each juice offers a unique pathway to a healthier heart. Embark on this flavorful voyage, where every sip is a step closer to optimal heart health.

Cardio Care: Pomegranate, Beetroot, and Walnut Wonder

2 servings | 10 mins | 0 mins

Equipment

Blender, knife, strainer

Ingredients

- 1 large pomegranate (seeds removed)
- 1 medium beetroot (peeled and chopped)
- 10 walnuts

Nutritional information:
170 calories; 4g protein; 30g carbohydrates; 7g fat; 6g fiber; 0mg cholesterol; 58mg sodium; 510mg potassium.

Directions

1. Combine pomegranate seeds, chopped beetroot, and walnuts in a blender.
2. Process until you reach a smooth consistency.
3. Use a strainer to filter out any remaining chunks.
4. Pour into glasses and enjoy immediately.

Benefits*: Dive deep into a cardiovascular wellness experience with this dynamic mix. Pomegranates, armed with antioxidants, battle oxidative stress. Beets, full of nitrates, champion optimal blood pressure, while walnuts, rich in Omega-3s, support artery flexibility and function.*

Vital Ventricle: Blueberry, Spinach, and Chia Seed Symphony

2 servings | 12 mins | 0 mins

Equipment

Blender, spoon

Ingredients

- 1 cup blueberries
- 1 cup spinach leaves (washed)
- 1 tablespoon chia seeds

Nutritional information:
140 calories; 3g protein; 28g carbohydrates; 4g fat; 8g fiber; 0mg cholesterol; 45mg sodium; 290mg potassium.

Directions

1. Add blueberries, spinach leaves, and chia seeds to the blender.
2. Blend until achieving a velvety-smooth mixture.
3. Serve immediately in chilled glasses.

***Benefits**: A harmony of heart-healthy heroes! Blueberries, packed with antioxidants, combat cellular damage. Spinach provides essential minerals and vitamins to fortify heart health. Meanwhile, chia seeds offer Omega-3 fatty acids, which further bolster cardiovascular well-being.*

Pulse Protector: Kiwi, Grape, and Olive Oil Oasis

Equipment

2 servings | 10 mins | 0 mins

Blender, spoon

Ingredients

- 2 ripe kiwis (peeled and sliced)
- 1 cup of red grapes
- 1 tablespoon of extra virgin olive oil

Nutritional information:
158 calories; 2g protein; 25g carbohydrates; 7g fat; 4g fiber; 0mg cholesterol; 5mg sodium; 420mg potassium.

Directions

1. Place kiwi slices, grapes, and olive oil into the blender.
2. Blend until smooth and well-mixed.
3. Pour into glasses and enjoy.

***Benefits**: Kiwis are a powerhouse of Vitamin C and E, aiding in reducing the risk of chronic diseases, including cardiovascular disease. Grapes, with their rich resveratrol content, promote heart health by improving blood flow. Olive oil, abundant in monounsaturated fats, has been known to manage LDL cholesterol levels, playing a critical role in heart protection.*

Rhythmic Radiance: Strawberry, Acai, and Oat Milk Rendezvous

Equipment

Blender

2 servings | 12 mins | 0 mins

Directions

1. Combine strawberries, acai berries, and oat milk in a blender.
2. Blend until creamy and smooth.
3. Serve immediately for a refreshing treat.

Ingredients

- 1 cup strawberries (washed and hulled)
- 2 tablespoons acai berry powder or puree
- 1 cup oat milk

Nutritional information:
145 calories; 3g protein; 29g carbohydrates; 3g fat; 5g fiber; 0mg cholesterol; 60mg sodium; 380mg potassium.

Benefits: *Strawberries brim with anthocyanins, benefiting heart health and blood pressure regulation. Acai berries offer a wealth of antioxidants, crucial for reducing oxidative stress, while oat milk delivers beta-glucans, known to manage cholesterol levels, ensuring your heart dances to a healthy beat.*

Circulation Charm: Orange, Ginger, and Green Tea Tango

Equipment

2 servings 10 mins 5 mins

Blender, juicer, teapot

Ingredients

- Juice of 2 oranges
- 1-inch piece of ginger, peeled and grated
- 1 cup brewed green tea (cooled)

Nutritional information:
60 calories; 1g protein; 14g carbohydrates; 0.5g fat; 2g fiber; 0mg cholesterol; 2mg sodium; 300mg potassium.

Directions

1. Make the green tea, then let it cool.
2. In a blender, combine orange juice, grated ginger, and cooled green tea.
3. Blend until smooth and serve immediately.

***Benefits**: Oranges are renowned for their vitamin C content, which supports healthy blood vessels. Ginger aids in blood circulation, while green tea's antioxidants, especially catechins, help prevent cell damage and reduce inflammation, vital for heart health.*

Artery Ally: Avocado, Broccoli, and Lemon Liaison

Equipment

Blender

2 servings | 12 mins | 0 mins

Directions

1. Add avocado, broccoli, and lemon juice to the blender.
2. Blend until smooth.
3. Serve immediately for a creamy, nutrient-packed treat.

Ingredients

- 1 ripe avocado, pitted and scooped
- 1 cup of broccoli florets
- Juice of 1 lemon

Nutritional information:
180 calories; 4g protein; 16g carbohydrates; 12g fat; 8g fiber; 0mg cholesterol; 25mg sodium; 650mg potassium.

***Benefits**: Avocados contain monounsaturated fats that are heart-healthy, along with potassium, which aids in managing blood pressure. Broccoli is rich in fiber, antioxidants, and vitamin K, promoting heart health. Lemon adds a dose of vitamin C, which is vital for arterial health.*

Beat Booster: Raspberry, Almond, and Turmeric Tonic

Equipment

Blender

2 servings | 10 mins | 0 mins

Ingredients

- 1 cup raspberries
- 10 almonds (soaked for easier blending)
- 1/2 teaspoon turmeric powder

Nutritional information:
110 calories; 3g protein; 12g carbohydrates; 6g fat; 5g fiber; 0mg cholesterol; 2mg sodium; 350mg potassium.

Directions

1. In a blender, combine raspberries, almonds, and turmeric.
2. Blend until smooth, adding water for desired consistency.
3. Pour into glasses and serve chilled.

***Benefits**: Raspberries offer a dose of heart-healthy fiber and essential vitamins. Almonds bring in vitamin E and monounsaturated fats, supporting heart health. Turmeric, with its curcumin content, has anti-inflammatory properties beneficial for the cardiovascular system.*

Heartbeat Harmony: Cherry, Flaxseed, and Hibiscus Hug

Equipment

2 servings | 10 mins | 5 mins

Blender, strainer

Ingredients

- 1 cup cherries (pitted)
- 1 tablespoon ground flaxseed
- 1 cup brewed hibiscus tea (cooled)

Nutritional information:
100 calories; 2g protein; 22g carbohydrates; 3g fat; 4g fiber; 0mg cholesterol; 8mg sodium; 270mg potassium.

Directions

1. Brew the hibiscus tea and let it cool.
2. In a blender, combine cherries, ground flaxseed, and cooled hibiscus tea.
3. Blend until smooth, then strain and serve immediately.

***Benefits**: The abundance of anti-inflammatory and antioxidant qualities in cherries can help reduce the incidence of heart issues. Flaxseeds are rich in omega-3 fatty acids, enhancing heart health. Hibiscus contributes to lower blood pressure levels, which is vital for cardiovascular well-being.*

Vascular Vigor: Apple, Kale, and Black Seed Bliss

2 servings | 12 mins | 0 mins

Equipment

Juicer

Ingredients

- 2 apples, cored and sliced
- 1 cup of kale leaves
- 1 teaspoon black seed oil

Nutritional information:
120 calories; 2g protein; 28g carbohydrates; 3g fat; 5g fiber; 0mg cholesterol; 25mg sodium; 350mg potassium.

Directions

1. Using a juicer, extract juice from the apples and kale leaves.
2. Stir in black seed oil.
3. Serve immediately.

***Benefits**: Apples have soluble fiber, which can help lower cholesterol levels in the blood. Kale is a powerhouse of vitamins and antioxidants, crucial for heart health. Black seeds have thymoquinone, which possesses antioxidative properties supporting heart function.*

Pulse Potion: Mango, Collagen, and Cacao Nib Nectar

Equipment

Blender

2 servings | 10 mins | 0 mins

Directions

1. In a blender, combine mango, collagen powder, and cacao nibs.
2. Blend until smooth.
3. Pour into glasses and serve chilled.

Ingredients

- 1 ripe mango, peeled and pitted
- 1 tablespoon collagen powder
- 1 tablespoon cacao nibs

Nutritional information:
170 calories; 5g protein; 32g carbohydrates; 4g fat; 4g fiber; 0mg cholesterol; 12mg sodium; 420mg potassium.

Benefits: *Mangos are not only rich in vitamins but also in dietary fiber and antioxidants, which support heart function. Collagen may help maintain the integrity of blood vessels. Cacao nibs bring in flavonoids, which can improve heart health by promoting blood flow and reducing blood pressure.*

Heart Hugger: Cucumber, Omega-3-rich Fish Oil, and Mint Medley

Equipment

2 servings | 10 mins | 0 mins

Blender, strainer

Directions

1. In a blender, combine cucumber slices, fish oil, and mint leaves.
2. Blend until smooth, then strain for a finer consistency if desired.
3. Pour into glasses, garnish with a mint leaf, and serve immediately.

Ingredients

- 1 large cucumber, peeled and sliced
- 1 tablespoon Omega-3-rich fish oil
- A handful of fresh mint leaves

Nutritional information:
80 calories; 1g protein; 7g carbohydrates; 5g fat; 2g fiber; 0mg cholesterol; 10mg sodium; 260mg potassium.

***Benefits**: Cucumbers are low in calories but provide essential vitamins and minerals. Fish oil rich in omega-3 fatty acids has been shown to reduce inflammation and the risk of chronic illnesses such as heart disease. Mint adds not only a refreshing flavor but also contains beneficial antioxidants.*

Valve Vitality: Lemon, Garlic, and Carrot Cocktail

Equipment

Juicer

2 servings | 12 mins | 0 mins

Directions

1. Using a juicer, extract juice from the lemons and carrots.
2. Mix the lemon-carrot juice with the minced garlic in a pitcher.
3. Stir well and serve over ice. If desired, strain to remove garlic bits before serving.

Ingredients

- Juice of 2 lemons
- 1 garlic clove, minced
- 2 large carrots, peeled

Nutritional information:
60 calories; 1g protein; 14g carbohydrates; 0.5g fat; 3g fiber; 0mg cholesterol; 20mg sodium; 380mg potassium.

Benefits: *Lemons are a significant source of vitamin C, which has been linked to improved heart health. Garlic has been proven to benefit the heart by maintaining healthy blood vessels and reducing cholesterol levels. Carrots, rich in beta-carotene and fiber, can lower cholesterol levels and aid heart health.*

Mastering the 28-Day Meal Plan

Planning Ahead

Embarking on a transformative 28-day journey requires foresight and preparation. Understand the importance of setting clear intentions, making informed choices, and getting organized in advance. This will not only make the process smoother but also more enjoyable.

Grocery Lists and Prepping Ingredients

Begin your journey on the right foot by arming yourself with a comprehensive grocery list tailored to each week's focus. Learn the art of prepping your ingredients efficiently, ensuring freshness, saving time, and reducing waste.

Weekly Snapshots

Week 1: Introduction and Ease-In

A gentle start, introducing the body to the juice cleanse.

DAY	CATEGORY	JUICE RECIPE
1	Detox and Cleanse Juices	Purity Punch: Pineapple, Ginger, and Kale Symphony
2	Weight Management Juices	Lean Lush: Grapefruit, Kale, and Cayenne Combo
3	Immunity Boosters	Defense Dynamo: Kiwi, Spinach, and Ginger Groove
4	Energy Enhancers	Dynamic Drive: Green Apple, Spinach, and Ginger Gust
5	Digestive Aids	Digestive Delight: Pineapple, Ginger, and Mint Mingle
6	Skin and Beauty Blends	Radiance Reviver: Strawberry, Aloe Vera, and Lime Liaison
7	Mind and Mood Modulators	Clarity Cocktail: Blueberry, Spinach, and Lavender Liaison

Week 2: Deepening the Detox and Focus on Nutrients

A gentle start, introducing the body to the juice cleanse.

DAY	CATEGORY	JUICE RECIPE
8	Mind and Mood Modulators	Calm & Collected: Pineapple, Banana, and Ashwagandha Concerto
9	Heart Health Helpers	Cardio Care: Pomegranate, Beetroot, and Walnut Wonder
10	Immunity Boosters	Protection Potion: Blueberry, Lemon, and Echinacea Essence
11	Detox and Cleanse Juices	Mellow Mender: Melon, Grapefruit, and Basil Blend
12	Weight Management Juices	Metabolic Majesty: Pineapple, Celery, and Turmeric Twist
13	Immunity Boosters	Vitality Verve: Green Apple, Spinach, and Rosehip Rally
14	Energy Enhancers	Pep Power Potion: Watermelon, Basil, and Chia Seed Symphony

Week 3: Intensifying Immunity Boosts

Further enhancing the body's immune system with powerful ingredients.

DAY	CATEGORY	JUICE RECIPE
15	Digestive Aids	Belly Bliss Brew: Papaya, Lemon, and Chamomile Combo
16	Skin and Beauty Blends	Glowing Grace: Kiwi, Cucumber, and Rose Water Rhapsody
17	Mind and Mood Modulators	Serenity Squeeze: Mango, Chamomile, and Almond Milk Symphony
18	Energy Enhancers	Energize Elixir: Blackberry, Orange, and Mint Mingle
19	Heart Health Helpers	Vital Ventricle: Blueberry, Spinach, and Chia Seed Symphony
20	Weight Management Juices	Trim Tonic: Pomegranate, Beetroot, and Mint Marvel
21	Immunity Boosters	Shielding Splash: Strawberry, Basil, and Elderberry Euphoria

Week 4: Reflect, Revitalize, and Rejuvenate

A week to rejuvenate, focus on holistic health, and prepare the body to end the juice plan.

DAY	CATEGORY	JUICE RECIPE
22	Detox and Cleanse Juices	Glowing Gusher: Green Apple, Fennel, and Aloe Vera Alliance
23	Weight Management Juices	Trim Tonic: Pomegranate, Beetroot, and Mint Marvel
24	Energy Enhancers	Zest Zenith: Blueberry, Acai, and Lime Lush
25	Digestive Aids	Gastric Grace: Mango, Turmeric, and Flaxseed Fusion
26	Skin and Beauty Blends	Silky Skin Sip: Peach, Avocado, and Almond Milk Medley
27	Mind and Mood Modulators	Focus Fusion: Green Apple, Kale, and Matcha Mix
28	Heart Health Helpers	Pulse Protector: Kiwi, Grape, and Olive Oil Oasis

These weekly themes offer an organized approach and might help participants better understand the progression and purpose of each week. Again, a reminder: always consult with a healthcare provider or nutritionist before starting any significant dietary changes or juice cleanses.

Conclusion

Your Continued Journey to Health

As we wrap up this enlightening journey through "Juicing for Beginners: Crafting Fresh Blends to Target Weight and Elevate Physical Well-being," let's reflect on the path we've trodden. We set out on this journey not only to grasp juicing as a method, but also to comprehend its potential to transform our health.

Revisiting Our Voyage

At the very start, we unearthed the wonders of fresh produce, understanding how the essence of fruits and vegetables, when transformed into juice, becomes an elixir for our bodies. From there, we navigated the intricate landscapes of blending techniques, equipment choices, and the profound impacts of various ingredients on our health. Each chapter offered a step closer to mastering the art and science of juicing, guiding you toward creating bespoke blends tailored to your personal health goals.

But beyond the how-tos and recipes, this book served as a testament to the transformative power of natural nutrition. It highlighted the promise of a lifestyle where we prioritize our bodies, giving them the nourishment they deserve. The myriad of benefits, from weight management to amplified physical vitality, stands as evidence of the wonders of this age-old yet freshly relevant practice.

Your Next Steps

The journey doesn't end as you flip this last page. It's just the beginning. Knowledge, they say, is potent only when applied. You now possess a treasure trove of insights, tips, and recipes. The onus is on you to harness this wisdom, integrate juicing into your daily regimen, and witness the metamorphosis in your health.

And as you continue this endeavor, remember that, like every skill, mastery in juicing comes with practice. Don't be disheartened by initial missteps or less-than-perfect blends. With each glass, you're not just consuming nutrients but also growing in your understanding and appreciation of this beautiful craft.

Your Voice Matters

This book was crafted with fervor and meticulous attention to guide beginners like you in their juicing journey. If the insights shared have enriched your life and nudged you toward better health, your feedback is invaluable. Please consider leaving a review on Amazon. Your words can inspire others, just as you were inspired, to embark on this transformative journey to optimal health.

Here's to a future radiant with health, vibrancy, and the delightful symphony of nature's best flavors in every glass. Cheers to your continued journey to health!

Index

Printed in Great Britain
by Amazon

32242152R00079